PLANNING & DESIGNING

L·I·G·H·T·I·N·G

PLANNING & DESIGNING

L·I·G·H·T·I·N·G

EDWARD EFFRON

Little, Brown and Company
Boston   Toronto

Library of Congress Catalog Card No. 87-81284

First American Edition

Planning and Designing Lighting
was conceived, edited and designed by
Frances Lincoln Limited, Apollo Works, 5 Charlton King's Road,
London NW5 2SB

*Published simultaneously in Canada
by Little, Brown & Company (Canada) Limited*

Typeset in Hong Kong by Best-set Typesetter Ltd.

Printed in Hong Kong

C·O·N·T·E·N·T·S

I·N·T·R·O·D·U·C·T·I·O·N

In the sixteen years that I have been designing with light, I am struck by how little most people know about the subject. We give light very little thought, we take it for granted – and yet we are universally affected by it all the time.

My reasons for writing this book could be described as essentially selfish. I'm assuming that if you, my potential clients, have more understanding and appreciation of light, I won't have to work so hard to convince you of its importance and of the need to spend money on it.

The power of light I want this book to demystify the subject, to make you appreciate lighting for what it is: light, which can occupy your space without obstructing it, is your only flexible design element. If you so choose, and with a little active participation, lighting can transform your room. You can alter color, make light brighter or dimmer, change its direction, its focus, and the size of the area illuminated. Your light can be soft or hard, and you can mix all these components in any proportion you like.

The power of light to attract and to make exciting statements is already being exploited by retailers and by club and restaurant owners. How daringly you use light in your own home is limited only by your imagination, your budget, and energy consciousness.

Light alters mood You have probably been depressed by a gloomy day before now, and scientific studies have shown that some people who suffer from depressions during the winter can be cured simply by the addition of extra light to their homes. On the other hand, bright sunny days tend to lift your spirits, and people are often favorably described as having 'sunny' dispositions. Good lighting in the home can have the same positive effect on you as bright natural light.

You may already realize that light affects your mood and general well-being, as well as your ability to work effectively and efficiently. An increased awareness of this is a good beginning, but it is not enough. It does not mean that most people have any better understanding of what light is. I hope the information in this book will change that.

People's increased awareness of light – as they are confronted with it in discotheques, restaurants, night-clubs, and shop windows – has led to an increased demand for 'lighting'. Manufacturers have responded accordingly. There now exists equipment to fulfil any requirement, solve any problem, and suit almost anyone's taste.

Yet I want this book to be above all about light, not just about beautiful and expensive light fixtures. Of course, a fixture influences the character of the light emerging from it; but in the end, no matter how expensive, a fixture is merely the means of conducting electricity, and a way of securing the lamp (or bulb). It is the lamp that emits the light.

Money into light Light and electricity have a parasitic relationship. Light is your design tool and electricity is something that it eats, and which also costs money. 'Goodness, wasn't the cost of the lighting included in the electrical estimate?' clients ask. Sometimes I think they expect artificial light to be free, as sunlight is. It certainly shouldn't have been included in the electrical budget. Your lighting needs to have a separate budget allocated to it, in the same way as you would work out a budget for your other fittings such as your kitchen equipment or your flooring.

As a lighting designer I have to convince you that any extra or unanticipated costs of lighting are well worth it, if only in terms of the increased enjoyment of your home. On the whole, 'good' lighting means more lighting, and perhaps this may require an initial investment higher than you expect. On the other hand, compared with what you may be spending on the rest of your decor, money spent on lighting is still a relatively inexpensive way of improving or redesigning your home.

Above all, good lighting does not have to mean higher running costs. Properly planned, managed, and looked after, good lighting can actually cost less to maintain than poor lighting overused ineffectively.

Indirect ceiling light combined with diffused table lamps give minimal glare, allowing a clear view of the city skyline.

We have come a long way from the time when a switch by the door and a fixture hanging from the center of the ceiling provided all the lighting for that room. But we have still not come far enough.

When it comes to 'doing up' your home, the element you know least and yet still most constantly use is your light. Because light and electricity are the least understood, and physically one of the last elements to be installed, time and again lighting is the first thing to go by the board. But saying you'll get round to doing the lighting later is the same as saying you'll never do it.

Anyone who has lived through building or renovation knows that, once the contractors have gone, the last thing you ever want to do is to get them back again. I want to try and make you see that shortchanging your lighting is the exact equivalent of cutting off your nose to spite your face.

After all, think how involved you get in choosing the colors, fabrics, furniture, fittings, and finishes in your home. Yet, when the sun goes down, the only way you see, enjoy, and create an environment for all this carefully chosen decor is through your lighting. You may be prepared to spend thousands of dollars on 'doing up' your house, so why then begrudge spending hundreds on lighting it? The answer is that light is too mysterious, and people shy away from becoming involved with it.

Energy conservation Converting electrical energy into light energy is a pretty inefficient process. Fluorescent light is far more energy-efficient than the incandescent light usually found in homes. For instance, if all the lighting in America were fluorescent, apparently forty, one-thousand-megawatt power plants would be freed to fulfil other energy needs.

This, of course, is seeing the subject in terms only of quantity of light, not quality. At what point you are prepared to trade quality of light for efficiency is a personal decision.

Future trends Not only is lighting itself quite a new design discipline, it is developing at an accelerating speed. New, improved, or different tools are being made available all the time. To keep abreast of all the changes requires immense effort, but is also a very exciting challenge.

Lighting's future undoubtedly lies in the development of improved and more efficient light sources. There will also be advances in the way light can be transmitted. At the moment, wherever you put the lamp is where you get the light. Using fiber optics, light can travel through a small rod and come out somewhere else – that is how doctors see inside the body. More practical fixtures will be developed on these lines, as well as those using mirrors and lenses to distribute the light from a single source in many directions.

Having said all this, I feel it would be unfair for me – if not impossible – to give you a magic formula for lighting a room, and I don't attempt to do so anywhere in this book. Instead, my aim throughout is to stimulate you to become consciously aware of light's influence on all you see around you; and I have tried to demystify some of the basic properties of light, as well as some basic tools, so that you can recognize your own lighting preferences, and either recreate them yourself, or be able to communicate what you want to someone else.

AUTHOR'S —ACKNOWLEDGMENTS—

To all of my friends who accurately predicted this book would take twice as long as I had anticipated, thanks for the encouraging warning. And had it not been for my editor, Sybil del Strother, the book might have taken three times as long. I am grateful for her prodding, probing, and guidance through the potholes of publishing.

To my art editor, Judith Robertson, thanks for a willing supply of erasers and the desire to make it right. And thanks to Steve Wooster for his design input, and to Anne Fraser for her never-ending picture research.

My London-based sister and brother-in-law, by running the best *pensione* in London – breakfast and dinner included – turned transatlantic necessity into pleasure.

Thankyou Dennis and Li Weinreich of Videosonics Studio for graciously giving me their conference room as a London office.

And thanks to the many people in the lighting industry, both manufacturers and practitioners – who were so giving of their encouragement, information, and knowledge – particularly Janet Turner of Concord and William Blitzer of Lightolier.

Finally, thanks to Karla, whose support kept our relationship going in spite of my discovery of the word processor/computer.

W·H·A·T IS L·I·G·H·T ?

☐ Light is the sum of many parts

☐ How those parts contribute to visual perception

☐ Color is light and light is color

☐ Reflection: what is seen is only what is bounced

back to the eye

☐ Shadow: the clue to interpretation of dimension

☐ Contrast: what makes it possible to

tell one thing from another

☐ Manipulating these properties alters

the visual impact of a space

P·R·O·P·E·R·T·I·E·S O·F L·I·G·H·T

If you wake up in an unfamiliar room in the middle of the night in the pitch-black dark, you will probably be disorientated. This is because you rely on your visual perception for the vast majority of the information you absorb from the world around you. With no light, you have no visual perception. Only with light can you see. So it follows that altering the nature of the light will change the way you 'see' things.

When you think about this it seems obvious – but probably you have never given the subject much thought. We take light totally for granted. Every waking minute we are bathed in it, subjected to it,

The cosy, inviting interior above, bathed in the warmth of incandescent light, is designed to attract the onlooker.

surrounded – indeed bombarded – by it. Even in sleep dreams are lit, often in color. Yet because the eye and brain are so forgiving, we have great tolerance for bad lighting. If light shapes all we see, knowing how to control it can help you to reshape your environment, or your perception of it.

CHARACTERISTICS — OF LIGHT —

Before you can control light, you need to know about its various properties. What stimulates the eye is a small piece of the electro-magnetic spectrum (see below), known as visible light. All light has identifiable characteristics – color, distribution, direction, intensity – and will be somewhere between perfectly focused (hard-edged) and non-focused (soft-edged).

If you place a small square of grey paper on a large piece of the same paper, you will not be able to distinguish the small square. To see it, you have to manipulate the attributes of light. You can elevate the square so that it casts a shadow; you can change its color (either by painting it or by using 'colored' light); you can direct more light on to it so as to alter the contrast. Changing the contrast will make the small square appear brighter (as well as lighter in color) than the large piece of paper. If you don't

want to add more light to the small square, you can change its reflective quality. Assuming for the moment that the paper is matt, you can give the small square a high gloss finish and cause it to reflect more light than the large piece of paper, making it more easily visible.

Consider your home – look at it by day and by night. It will not appear at all the same, because the light is different. In most cases daylight, transmitted through vertical windows, lights things from the side, while electric light, on the other hand, is emitted, and usually lights from above. The shadows cast by each differ both in shape and quality. Daylight is more intense, and its color composition is very different.

Courses in lighting are relatively new to formal education. They are rarely available to interested members of the public. Even professionals get few opportunities to experiment with the hundreds of fixtures and light sources (lamps) in varying spaces. Stores that sell fixtures are seldom staffed with knowledgeable help, while their displays make it impossible for you to view one lamp or fixture at a time.

But since all your time is spent in light, perhaps experience can be your guide – if not hands-on experience, then observed experience. The way anything appears is a result of the light that falls on it. You need to work backwards from what you are looking at to the light source that revealed it.

All good designers share one thing in common, a highly developed observational skill. Like them, you need to begin observing your world with an eye that asks, 'Why does that appear as it does?' Each day you have the chance to look at lighting in different places – offices, restaurants, friends' homes, schools, trains, theatres, and so on. At the risk of being rude, you may have to look behind valances, under shelves, and into coves. If you can see something, there must be a light source.

Once you begin to recognize lighting equipment and lamps, the best place to identify them and get information on their performance is in manufacturers' catalogues.

With patient and practised observation you should eventually be able to manipulate light to achieve the effect you want.

THE ELECTRO-MAGNETIC SPECTRUM

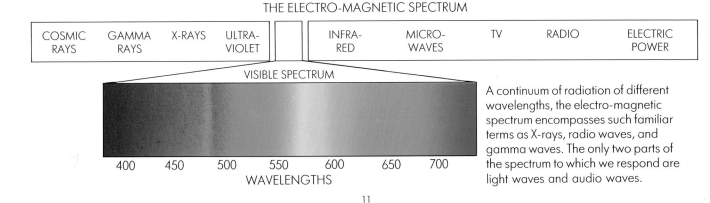

A continuum of radiation of different wavelengths, the electro-magnetic spectrum encompasses such familiar terms as X-rays, radio waves, and gamma waves. The only two parts of the spectrum to which we respond are light waves and audio waves.

C·O·L·O·R

I mention on page 11 that the eye is stimulated by the part of the electromagnetic spectrum known as 'visible light'. Visible light itself is composed of many colors. The familiar prism, illustrated right, shows that sunlight is a rainbow of colors (or wavelengths), together perceived to be 'white' light

—COLOR PERCEPTION—

The perception of color is one of the most amazing attributes of the human eye. It is also one of the most baffling and frustrating. Scientists have developed several so-called 'accurate' ways of describing color. They include the Color Triangle, the Ostwald Color System, and the Munsell Color System. But, for all these methods, consider how many everyday color descriptions begin with 'sort of...' and/or end with 'ish'. It seems we must conclude that a simple and precise language for everyday color description has yet to be discovered and implemented.

Part of the problem is that the way people see color is the result of the brain's interpretation. Each individual's perception is subjective and slightly different. So, no matter how accurately science measures colors and the color of light, when it comes to personal design decisions your eye and your brain will be the final judges.

The color measuring systems mentioned above all refer to the colors of objects – pigment, or paint. In many ways it is paint manu-

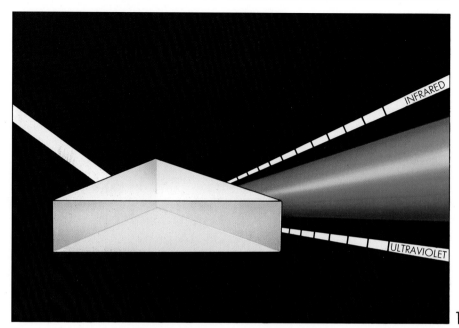

facturers who have helped us to overcome our verbal inadequacy, by making available to the general public thousands of samples in the form of little 'colored chips'. These chips have become a common ground for color communication in the decoration of homes, even though the small print says that no guarantee is made that the match will be absolute.

Matching color and light source
Because perception of color is so subjective, the only really sound advice is to make all decisions about your color schemes under the lighting conditions you intend to have. You are then in no danger of being unexpectedly disillusioned. An example will quickly make this clear. Imagine that you visit a showroom and buy a

beautiful leather sofa, the color of burgundy wine. Months later it arrives, and you rush home from work, only to find what now looks like a beautiful greyed, reddish-brown leather sofa. A night sleepless with disappointment anticipates angry phone calls and threats. But the next morning the sofa looks as you remember it. Consternation leads to deduction: the color of the sofa is an exotic blend of blues and reds, with overtones and shades of warm earth; you bought it from a bright, daylit showroom, but you intended to enjoy it after a hard day's work – at night, in artificial light.

Different colored light sources
All rainbows are not the same. The colors that make up sunlight only make up sunlight. All other sources

of light – incandescent, halogen, fluorescent, and so on – have their own distinctive rainbows of wavelengths.

In addition, all these rainbows have different size color bands (expressing different wavelength energies). They may be stronger in blue, weaker in green, very short of red, or any possible combination. Even within daylight, there are huge spectral differences. Depending on whether you bought your sofa at noon, at dusk, or on a cloudy, rainy day, it would have looked different in the showroom.

It should now be obvious that your sofa cannot be described as having a consistent color if you have to see it in different-colored light sources.

—1—

This prism shows how sunlight can be broken up into a 'rainbow' of colors, which all together are perceived by the eye as white light.

—2—

These five color samples demonstrate how differently you perceive color under different light sources. (You must allow for the fact that photographic film and the developing and printing processes have slightly affected the look of the colors.)

a This represents daylight of 5500 Kelvin (see p. 91). Its spectrum of colors is well balanced and will serve as the reference. **b** This light source is a 150-watt A lamp, 2600 Kelvin. Compared with **a**, the reds are slightly richer, while the blues and greys are warmer, with a reddish cast. **c** This

2

a – DAYLIGHT

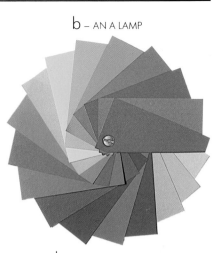

b – AN A LAMP

c – HALOGEN LAMP

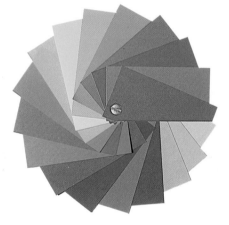

d – A FLUORESCENT LAMP

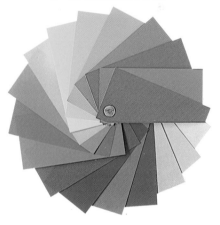

e – A MERCURY VAPOR LAMP

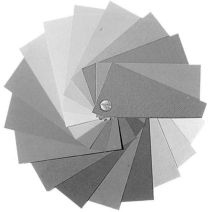

source rates 3050 Kelvin. The warm colors appear similar to the way they look in **b**, but the cool colors have a crispness approximating more to **a**. **d** The fluorescent source is cool white, with a Kelvin temperature of 4200. The red colors are compressed or 'muddied'. On the other hand, yellow and orange look close to **a**, and the blue and grey tones are enhanced. **e** This particular mercury vapor lamp has a Kelvin temperature of 3300, close to that of halogen. The color rendering, however, is decidedly poor.

Warm light and cool light For general purposes, it is adequate to over-simplify the color characteristics of a light source. (For examples of more precise, scientific measuring systems and when and how they are used, see page 91 of the Lamps and Fixtures section.) Light sources are divided into 'cool' (towards blue) and 'warm' (towards red).

Daylight at sunrise and sunset are very warm; at noon the light is cool, and even cooler if the sky is overcast; while light from a clear blue, northwest sky is cold. Which of these daylight colors do you prefer?

In homes, the most commonly used electric light source is the incandescent lamp, which is considered warm. On a cloudy day, light from a reading lamp seems very yellow compared with any daylight coming through the window.

In fact, the chart on page 80 confirms that the spectral make-up of incandescent light is very weak in blue light and strong on red. Sun and sky light are strong in both (this is why the exotic color blend of the leather sofa is more accurately rendered in the daylit showroom than under incandescent light at home).

Subjective color associations are probably more important than absolute, objective color evaluation. Surveys show that, where appearance is important, people prefer light sources rich in red, because they impart a healthy, rosy complexion to Caucasian skin. People also prefer low-level or dim light to be warm in tone. Perhaps this harks back to the reassuring glow of a fire, or to the intimacy of candlelight.

On the other hand, where high levels of illumination are desired, most people tend to prefer cool light. Perhaps this is because cool daylight is associated with nine-to-five working conditions. Traditionally, fluorescent light was very cool, with a poor red spectrum; this no longer has to be true, but people are still reluctant to use it in their homes, except in the more work-oriented areas such as kitchens, bathrooms, studies, or nurseries.

Certainly, there is no longer any color excuse not to use fluorescent light in the home, wherever its linear, diffuse quality is appropriate. Most manufacturers now offer lamps across the whole spectral range, with various 'rainbow' patterns. There are fluorescent lamps to complement all color schemes.

The eye's color memory You are subjected to so many different-colored light sources, with no object appearing exactly the same under any two sources; how is it that you are not constantly in a state of subtle color disorientation? The answer lies in a further dynamic eye/brain process that endows you with color memory and predetermined color expectations.

For example, you know and anticipate a tomato to be red. But if you shine green light (which has no red wavelengths) on a tomato, it will appear very grey; the pigment absorbs the green, and there is no red to reflect back to your eye. That is the extreme case. In any conditions less than extreme, your color memory tends to fill in the missing wavelengths, and your built-in color asso-

ciations mean that you do not even notice the change in light source. Whether you see it in daylight, rich in red, or under certain fluorescents that are weak in red, you know that a tomato is red.

Within reason, the eye and brain adjust colors for you. When you move from a coolly lit white kitchen to a warmly glowing dining table, you are very aware of a change in color contrast. Suddenly more relaxed, you adjust quickly and unthinkingly to the changed color of your environment. Under both lights the tomato is still red.

Thinking about light colors Have you chosen the colors of your decorative scheme for their value in both daylight and artificial light? Or is one source of light more important than the other?

Look at an example: a white sparkling kitchen might be very crisp in daylight, but at night, in incandescent light, it could have a drab, yellowish feel to it. Now, halogen light, while still a form of incandescent, has an enhanced blue spectrum, and so is a cooler light source than an ordinary incandescent lamp. This makes it a more appropriate light source to use with whites, greys, and blues. But, like standard incandescent lamps, halogen lamps yellow or 'go warm' when dimmed.

Artificial light is meant to enhance your interiors. It will bring out your chosen palette of colors, just as long as you put a little thought and planning into matching the colors around you with the colors of the light sources you have decided they will be seen in.

R·E·F·L·E·C·T·I·O·N

If you look directly at the sun – not a good idea – what you see are burning gases, not light. When you look at an artificial light source, you still do not see light: in a clear lamp you see the tungsten wire filament heated by electricity until it glows: in a pearlized lamp, the glass jacket, or bulb, is seen as a bright diffuser.

You do not see light itself, but only the end product of light. Nothing is visible until light strikes and *reflects* off something, anything. The narrow, intense beam of light in a nightclub is really only smoke, or fine dust particles, reflecting light within the angle of the source. The moon is not itself a light source: you see it only because it reflects the light of the sun.

You judge the amount of light a room has by how much is being reflected off the walls, ceiling, and floor, back to your eye. The reflectivity of a surface is a function of its material as well as its color (see chart, right).

QUALITIES OF REFLECTION

You unconsciously use the different qualities of reflection to define your environment. For example, you know instinctively if your kitchen worktop is wet, because the smooth shiny surface of water does not reflect light in the same way as your worktop does. Marble floors can be so highly polished and reflective that they appear wet and seem to have depth, like a pond.

Reflection allows you to differentiate between a puddle and a wet street. You can tell the fine fishbone from the white flesh of the fish, because the two reflect light differently. You know if something is dirty, because a fine layer of dust changes the way a surface reflects light.

Similarly, shiny white tiles reflect more light, and in a different way, than matt black paint does. In a dark room, lit only by a single spotlight, you are still aware of light reaching other areas of the room. How much depends on the reflectivity of the room's surfaces. Being a form of energy, light cannot just disappear, but continues to bounce around until it is all absorbed.

Indirect lighting This lighting technique, providing soft atmospheric light, depends on reflection from a ceiling. Cove lighting, uplighters mounted on the wall or floor, and table or floor lamps with open-topped shades all cast indirect

A room painted white, with one central light source, reflects more light than a similar room painted black. The chart below is a guide to the percentage of light hitting a color or surface that is reflected back to your eye.

There is a relationship between color and surface: for instance, matt white paint is less reflective than gloss white paint. Ceilings normally have the most reflectivity, floors the least, with walls somewhere in between.

REFLECTIVITY OF VARIOUS COLORS AND MATERIALS			
Colors	Per cent	Materials	Per cent
White	70–80	Maple	60
Light cream	70–80	Birch	60
Light yellow	55–65	Red brick	5–25
Light green	45–50	Concrete	15–40
Pink	45–50	Light oak	40
Sky-blue	40–45	Dark oak	15–20
Light grey	40–45	White enamel	65–75
Beige	25–35	Clear glass	6–8
Yellow ocher	25–35	Wood-fiber	
Light brown	25–35	cream boards	50–60
Olive green	25–35	Glazed white tiles	60–75
Orange	20–25		
Vermilion red	20–25	Dark walnut	15–20
Medium grey	20–25	Plaster	80
Dark green	10–15		
Dark blue	10–15	For comparison:	
Dark red	10–15	Carbon-black	
Dark grey	10–15	or black velvet	2–10
Navy blue	5–10	Glass/aluminium	
Black	4	mirror	95

The reflections of color and light bouncing off the glossy surfaces provide high-key interest and contribute to the above jacuzzi's exotic setting.

light. The technique works best when light-colored, matt-reflective surfaces are involved. If, for example, you decide to light a space indirectly, and the ceiling is painted a bright gloss yellow, the color and distribution of the indirect light will be influenced by the color and surface of the reflector (in this case the ceiling).

Luminance The reflectivity of a surface also influences how bright the surface itself seems to be. The quantitative term for this is luminance. The common term, brightness, is really a qualitative term of visual response, and can be influenced by external circumstances. For instance, a light blue wall in an otherwise white room will seem brighter than it would if the surrounding walls were dark blue, even though the measured luminance of the wall is the same in both circumstances.

—TRANSMISSION—

This is the opposite of reflection. You might assume that a clear glass window transmits all the light hitting it. In fact, only 80 to 90 per cent is transmitted, and the light that is not transmitted is reflected or absorbed. (Absorbed light is most often detected as heat – touch a sunny window.)

Materials that allow light to pass without appreciably scattering it are transparent, those that break up light are translucent (diffusers), and surfaces that pass no light are opaque. Dust on a window causes light to be scattered and changes the glass from a clear transparency to a more diffuse translucency.

——GLARE——

Any brightness/luminance that is greater than what your eye is adapted to can be defined as glare.

There are many degrees of glare. Driving off into the sunset may be a romantic image, but it often involves fighting 'blinding' glare, one so intense that for a short period of time nothing can be seen – like a flash bulb popping in your face. Other degrees of glare are 'disabling', 'discomforting', and 'annoying'. Everyone's tolerance of glare is different, but that does not mean it should have to be tolerated, especially if it occurs at home or work on a regular basis.

These different degrees of glare can occur in one of two ways, directly or indirectly.

Direct glare You should do your best to avoid any direct glare, which is excessive luminance in your field of view. The most common offender is the inadequately shielded lamp. Obviously a light source has a higher luminance than anything it is illuminating. If a bare lamp is in your normal line of view, which is assumed to be straight ahead, you should consider it glaring.

Recessed fittings where a bright lamp is too close to the ceiling opening are always a source of glare. Trying to light an entire room with a single central light source will prove glaring. A bright lampshade against a dark wall is not comfortable, although the same lampshade against a light wall would be acceptable. During the day, windows become very bright surfaces and, compared to the rest of the room – especially if the colors are dark or if daylight does not penetrate deeply – they are glaring. Blinds, curtains and tinted glass can lessen the glare of windows.

If you have problems with direct glare, you can attach louvres or barn doors (see page 129) to improve a fixture's cut-off angle or lamp shielding. Covering a fixture with a lens or diffuser spreads the brightness over a larger area, making it less offensive. However, lenses and diffusers also change the distribution and character of the light.

If you have exposed decorative lamps, a lot of dim ones are more comfortable than a few brighter ones. Simply dimming light sources may restore a non-glaring balance, but will probably also result in too little light for most practical purposes and not enough contrast or visual interest. More than one light source is almost always required.

Indirect or reflected glare An example of 'blinding' reflected glare would be to bounce the sun into someone's eyes using a mirror. As the victim of such foolery, your instinct would be to move away. Whether you realize it or not, you know that reflected glare can be avoided if you change your position so that the reflection no longer dazzles you.

Everyone has experienced glare from glossy magazine pages, and you know that to redirect the reflection you have to move – either the magazine, the light source, or your position. You may also have noticed that reflections off glossy surfaces actually conceal the surface's color – it appears 'white'.

A surprising number of headaches are the result of glare and the distortions people assume to avoid it. So, in planning your lighting, you want to minimize reflected glare. If you are using bright reflective materials, such as mirrors, glazed tiles, or gloss paint on smooth walls, you are providing potentially glaring surfaces. Surveying the room from the positions you usually occupy, try to determine whether any bright light will be reflected into your eyes.

Controlling reflected glare is especially important near work surfaces such as kitchen counters, which are often made of highly reflective materials like stainless steel, tiles, or plastic laminates. You should make sure that under-cabinet lights are shielded properly or diffused enough for their reflection not to be glaring.

Do not be discouraged by this from decorating your interiors with highly reflective materials – they are exciting. You only need to pay careful attention to lighting them. Remember, if you do it wrong it's glaring, but if you do it right people say 'it sparkles'.

S·H·A·D·O·W

Shadows are a fact of light. They occur when an obstacle is placed in the path of light. Beams of light travel in straight lines and cannot bend. Everything is an obstacle in light's path.

When observing an object, the light will reveal what it is you are looking at, be it a bowl of fruit or a piece of sculpture, but it is the shadow that will tell you about the object's size, shape, and spatial position. Binocular vision allows you to perceive depth and this, combined with experience of the environment, provides you with most of your information on size and shape. However, when viewing the world rendered in two dimensions (such as on film or in this book), you depend on shadows to interpret the scene. While you take this for granted, anyone who has lost depth perception certainly does not.

Flat lighting To understand shadows better, it helps to consider the effect their absence has on your perception of things. The best example of minimal shadow is the light on a completely cloudy, overcast day. This condition is known as 'flat' light. Often these days feel gloomy, the world lacks sparkle, things appear dull, and your spirits drop.

When examining yourself in your bathroom mirror flat lighting is complimentary, as all your features are revealed equally. On the other hand, when this type of light is used for your passport photo, it is rarely flattering. In a good portrait the

photographer will have successfully manipulated shadows to emphasize good features and diminish others.

Shadows have two qualities that can be controlled. The first is their direction or angle. Overhead lighting produces shadows in your eye sockets and is not flattering. The same overhead light grazing down a brick wall will reveal and enhance its texture. Conversely, 'flat' light can be facially flattering but would render the brick wall featureless. Objects classically appear more pleasing when their shadows come from light directed at a 45° to 60° angle.

The second controllable quality of shadow is its depth or density. The sun with its parallel rays gives the deepest and sharpest shadows. Of the artificial light sources, lamps with clear bulbs and tiny filaments, and fixtures using projector lenses, give the deepest shadows. The softest shadows are from indirect or bounced light, from fluorescent lamps, from fixtures that employ light-softening diffusers, and from frosted lamps with long filaments. Distance is also a factor: the closer the object to the shadowed surface, the sharper the shadow.

You associate steep angles and deep shadows with dramatic environments, while soft shadows are considered to be weak, tranquil, or romantic. In practice, the total effect and rendering of shadow depends on the interplay of all your light sources, as they reflect off the various surfaces of your room.

—1—

This picture illustrates flat lighting, coming from a light source shining from the same position as the camera.

—2—

A lensed projector placed directly above the sculpture produces deep dramatic shadows.

—3—

This shows the same light source as in **2**, now diffused. The shadows are softer and slightly more detail can be discerned.

—4—

The same lensed projector placed higher and to one side changes the appearance of the sculpture.

—5—

The lighting set-up is the same as in **4** except that the object is near a white wall. The sculpture's own shadow is evident, and the sculpture's shadowed side is weakened by light reflecting off the wall.

—6—

The same light source diffused (and consequently weakened) creates softer shadows.

—7—

All the room's light sources playing on the sculpture simultaneously lend a subtle feeling of depth and texture to the sculpture.

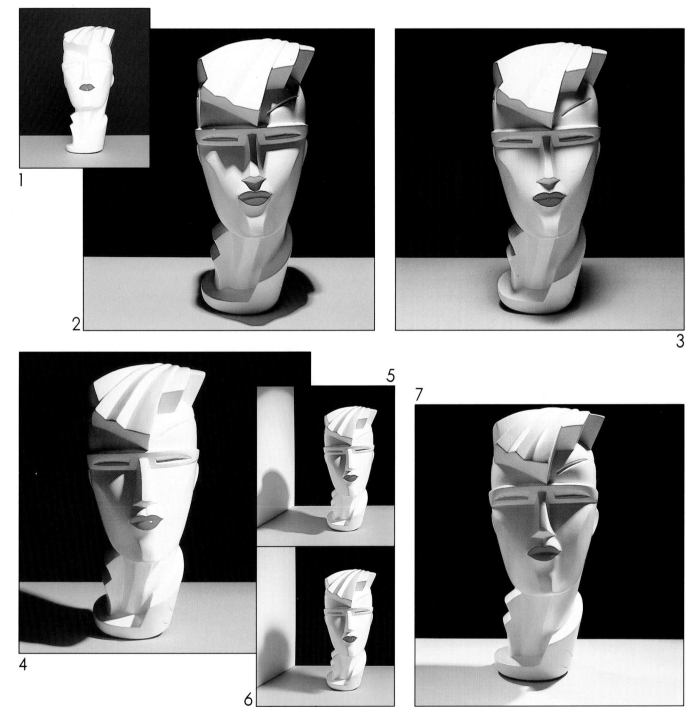

C·O·N·T·R·A·S·T

What the layman thinks of as contrast is termed 'brightness relationships' by the lighting community. It is the *relative brightness* or luminance of various surfaces, as well as their differing color values, that enables you to distinguish what it is you are looking at. It is the contrast of the black ink against the white page that is allowing you to distinguish letters and read this book.

In effect, the shadows of the three-dimensional world could just as easily be explained in terms of contrast. In two dimensions, such as this book, you perceive only contrast, which you then interpret as shadows.

Manipulating contrasts The ultimate example of contrast manipulation for effect might be a discotheque. Even if you eliminate the sound, the constant changes of light and color create an atmosphere of enormous contrasts and extreme visual stimulation.

Preparing for a dinner party by lighting your dining room with only candles or a few shafts of light produces a more exciting atmosphere, full of contrasts, than if the room were evenly washed by a central light. Try using accent or under-shelf light to punctuate objects on display; it makes them seem more interesting than if they were lit only by the general light of the room. A walk through a deep forest on a sunny day is visually more stimulating than the same walk taken on a dreary, overcast day.

Controlling contrasts To create visual interest in a space, you need to have 'pockets' of contrast. As a rule, very high contrast is associated with dramatic environments, like the discotheque. And you cannot create visual interest in a room with a single light source. Usually, the more dramatic the space, the more light sources and separate control you will need.

You do not need the same drama in work-oriented spaces, such as kitchens, but you do want visual stimulation, as it is found to relieve the eye and lessen fatigue. It could be that a nearby reflective surface does the trick; more often another circuit of lighting is required, such as a wall wash at one end of a kitchen opposite a small eating area.

In areas where exacting tasks (such as sewing or food preparation) or prolonged ones (perhaps reading, using a computer, or watching television) are done, controlling the contrast becomes especially important. In addition to the proper amount of light for the task (see the fc level chart on page 132), you want to control the background so that the task to background rato is 3:1. As your eye adapts to varying light levels automatically, high-contrast working light can lead to eye fatigue or headaches – say from the use of a reading light in an otherwise completely dark room.

Contrast ratios The eye is an amazing involuntary organ. It is constantly adjusting to varying levels of brightness, and can tolerate ratios as high as 1000:1 (say, a candle against a black background, or deep shadows in a sunlit forest). On the other hand, negative film can only handle contrast of 100:1, and television around 20:1; this in part explains why live viewing is more exciting than watching television is. A low-voltage spotlight in a dimly lit room can represent a contrast ratio of 125:1. Ratios of 70:1 or higher are called 'high key'.

Glare I have already talked about glare on page 17, defining it in terms of reflection. It is equally possible to define glare in terms of excessive contrast. The main distinction is that glare alters with your viewing position, while contrast does not. The reflector of a recessed fixture in a dark ceiling, while not a source of glare, may appear to have excessive contrast when compared with the same fixture in a white ceiling. A similar impression will be made by a table lamp with a light-colored, highly translucent shade if it is being looked at against a dark wall.

Inadequate contrast can be a problem too. When you read a newspaper, glare in the form of veiling reflections can reduce the amount of contrast between ink and paper. To maintain maximum contrast you should avoid reflection on your television, or computer or video screen.

In the garden on the right, the visual excitement of the foliage textures and colors is enhanced by the high contrast of dark night and bright light.

A·LT·E·R·I·N·G V·I·S·U·A·L I·M·P·A·C·T

By using two or more separately controlled lighting circuits in any given space, you can change somewhat the visual impression a particular room makes. Even small adjustments to a room's lighting can modify the look or feel of the space. Always desirable, this becomes particularly important when a room serves many different purposes. On the next three pages, two examples are given of how light can be used in this way.

In the kitchen below and right, light was needed for both working and dining. A suspended modular tube system has been installed with linear halogen lamps that give broad strokes of light. The system is further augmented by track that has been recessed into the walls around the perimeter of the room for accent lighting.

The kitchen on the right is well supplied with traditional under-shelf fluorescent tubes. Together with linear halogen lamps, these provide ample light with minimal shadows, suitable for both work surfaces and storage cupboards.

By dimming the work lights and turning on the low-voltage display spots located around the kitchen's perimeter, as shown far right, the mood is easily changed. The spots highlight the hanging pots and pans, as well as directing attention to the far end of the room, where the polycarbonate dome and tile wall are accented.

Lighting a space before its use and furniture plan are finalized is risky. Nothing was known in advance about the way this room would be used – the initial specification gave nothing apart from the dimensions, the reflective surface materials, and the color (white).

The lighting had to be versatile, but there was not enough information to provide for specific accent lights. Consequently, a modular tube system with linear halogen lamps was chosen, the same as the one shown and described on pages 22–3, incorporating six separate lighting circuits, each on a dimmer for maximum flexibility.

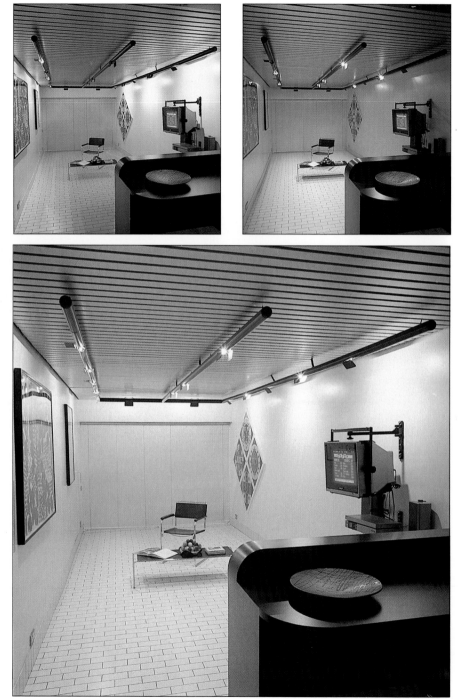

In the room above left, three circuits of light for wall washing help to expand an otherwise narrow space (3.3m or 10ft 10in). The reflective walls provide plenty of indirect light.

The harsh materials and bare feel make a warm atmosphere hard to achieve. However, keeping all lights off the walls, as shown above right, helps to create a sense of intimacy.

Bringing all the lights into play, as seen below, fills the room with a high level of illumination. The reflective surfaces combined with the halogen light source give a good quality work or playroom light with soft shadows.

R·O·O·M BY R·O·O·M

- ☐ An examination of every space in and around the house, with the lighting challenges each presents
- ☐ Entrances, halls and stairs, including paths, steps and doors
- ☐ Living rooms – art, plants and architectural features
- ☐ Kitchens and dining rooms – work surfaces, storage units and eating areas
- ☐ Bedrooms and children's rooms – reading lights, wardrobes and flexible lighting
- ☐ Bathrooms, including mirrors and showers
- ☐ Workrooms – task lighting
- ☐ One-room living
- ☐ Conservatories, exteriors and gardens

E·N·T·R·A·N·C·E·S

If first impressions are lasting, then the entrance to your house is a revealing feature. From a practical point of view the light should illuminate your caller, either directly or from reflected light. You should also light any pathway, although since the doorway itself is the most attracting feature, the path should be more dimly lit. The architecture may well dictate the type of fixture – a converted gaslamp in a Georgian house, perhaps, or a round opal glass cylinder in a modern house.

A bright light in the dark can cause too much contrast and seem glaring; generally soft lighting is more pleasant. You may find a single source playing on various architectural surfaces adequate, but several softer and dimmer sources are preferable. Light along the path should also be shielded from view to avoid glare. Tall poles with directional light, or fittings at knee height with general light, are suitable.

Any steps should be visible and can even have light built into them. You can use what lamps you like as long as their placement does not throw confusing shadows. With low lighting levels on steps and paths, you might want to make these surfaces more reflective or lighter in color than the surrounding areas, so that people are more easily guided along. (Visibility is the reason for white reflective stripes on pedestrian crossings.)

Concealed lighting If your entrance is covered, you have the option of concealing your lighting.

Glare is not a problem, since you have to look up above your head when at the door to be affected by it. The light will be more in evidence than the design of the fixture, so you can use simple fixtures. Alternatively, you can light covered entrances indirectly with a diffuse source, by bouncing light off the ceiling.

Dramatic lighting If the entrance to your house is grand, you might want to create a more dramatic impression. To this end you will find using a PAR lamp or other spotlight to aim the light straight down at your doorstep more effective than lighting your whole entrance. Similarly, if your door contains etched, bevelled, or stained-glass panels, using light inside the house to illuminate them has more impact than lighting them from outside in the ordinary way.

Weatherproof lamps and fixtures The degree to which your outdoor fixtures are exposed to the elements will determine how weatherproof they should be. Make sure you choose lamps that are still able to operate efficiently if the temperature drops very low. And remember that since outdoor fixtures are exposed to extra dirt and corrosion, you will need to maintain them more rigorously than indoor ones (see page 132).

Entrances to apartments Few landlords will object should you take the trouble to install some interesting lighting in a communal hallway. Be proud to say 'Mine is the third door on the right, the one with the pretty wall sconce next to it.'

A distinctive mood has been created for the secluded entranceway on the right by the variety and the density of its plant life. Contrasts in the textures and colors of the foliage are intensified by the effective lighting.

Fittings holding PAR 38 lamps have been positioned at a height designed to provide maximum illumination for the plants, without subjecting anyone walking along to direct glare. The lantern above the door at the end of the passage makes an inviting focal point for the arriving guest.

Several possible techniques for lighting an entrance are illustrated below. The 'period' fixtures on either side of the door and the two large globes, with diffuse lamps, are suggested as alternatives. The step lights could be used in conjunction with either or both.

H·A·L·L·S & S·T·A·I·R·S

The abstract spaces that link the rooms of your house together need to be lit as carefully as individual rooms – but this rarely happens.

—— ENTRANCE HALLS ——

Few – if any – tasks ever take place in the hall and little time is spent in it. It is the place where friends and guests are greeted, where their coats are taken and dealt with, and where they are made to feel comfortable – or not.

Since so little time is spent in the hall, you might not think it worth paying much attention to its lighting. But because it is such an abstract space, the entrance hall tends to reveal a lot about the tone of the house and its owners. Think a little about the psychology of its lighting and the moods you are interested in creating. More obviously, there may be objects you wish to highlight, or architecture that would look good –

without much furniture to distract the eye. True, the size does ultimately determine just how much time is spent in the hall. Even so, the eye responds to a great deal in a short swift glance.

Halls and corridors Halls that act as passageways to other rooms must be adequately lit for safe passage (the lowest accepted lighting level is 5–10 footcandles). This lighting level is fine unless you habitually

Two low-voltage display spotlights are the only source of light in the hallway on the left. As downlights, focused on the Grecian urns, they provide a degree of drama, while the high reflectivity of the floor materials bounces plenty of light around the rest of the hall. Notice how the eye is drawn through the doorway by the red wall beyond – the contrast in color is a particularly eye-catching aspect of this design.

Semi-recessed linear halogen fittings are in effect being used as wall washers in the hall on the right. Halogen is more flattering to the light tones of the color scheme than ordinary incandescent light; it also blends better with the daylight coming through the living-room windows. The overall feel is that of a very bright and sunny day, and this has been suitably reinforced by the artificial light.

enter the hall from a very bright space, in which case your eye needs some time to adapt to the lower light level.

Art is often displayed along corridors. Trying to 'accent light' specific works of art is hard, because the space limitations force you to put lights on one side of a hall, which is often unsatisfactory. Display halls need to have broad general illumination, which can be achieved with linear incandescent or fluorescent lamps, recessed, semi-recessed, or surface-mounted. You could also use a double wall washer (see page 106).

Long corridors often lend themselves to dramatic effects – for instance, pools of light can draw you along their length.

——STAIRS——

For safety, stairs should be lit to the same minimum footcandle (fc) levels as halls. Yet stairways are frequently overlooked, and have to make do with whatever light reflects off surfaces from other areas. If there is still enough light for you to see your way, this sort of oversight is acceptable. But often this is not the case.

At the very least, you should light the top and bottom stairs, as well as any intermediate landing, to distinguish them from adjacent floors.

When you are planning your stair lighting, make sure that no light shines directly in your eyes as you are going up or down the stairs – such direct glare could be hazardous. Staircases are often architecturally interesting: lighting them can add to your sense of receding or expanding space in the house.

Reflected light from sources elsewhere in the house provides even light for the spiral staircase above. In contrast, the adjustable accent lights placed around the perimeter of the upper landing are a source of visual interest. They have been deliberately directed so that they do not illuminate all the pictures evenly, with the effect of attracting the onlooker's attention to the lighting as much as the pictures.

In the photograph above right, an arc of downlights reinforces the division between the hall and the dining room, also clearly marked by the change in direction of the floorboards. The glossy finishes of the ceiling, the walls, and the wooden floor provide enough bounced light for the entire hall.

Another downlight illuminates the flower arrangement in the alcove, and a wall sconce on the living-room wall beyond is clearly visible through the darkened glass that forms the back of the alcove.

The stairwell on the far right is lit by linear fluorescent lamps. This provides a wide distribution of light, suitable for illuminating the art on the walls, and also accentuates the narrow stairway's linear nature.

In addition, an angled mirror-finish louvre shields the lamp from the person going upstairs (see detail), while the person coming down is actually reflected in the mirror finish.

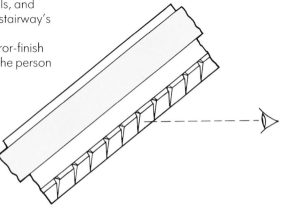

L·I·V·I·N·G R·O·O·M·S

The typical living room is a multi-functional space. Before attempting to light or relight it, ask yourself a number of questions about the way you use it.

How much time do you spend in it? Is it primarily for entertaining? Is it formal (no youngsters or animals allowed) or informal? Or do the rules change according to the time of day? Are any tasks performed in it (sewing, reading, television watching)? Are paintings and objects displayed in it? You probably know where you want all your furniture to be, and what the color scheme is. You should also consider the reflectivity of the walls, floor, and ceiling. If the room is used all day, does the transition from natural to artificial light need some thought?

Depending on your answers and the budget, a good deal of lighting can go into a living room, where a lot of tasks are usually performed and a high degree of visual interest is desirable. General lighting need not be uniform and for interest's sake should not be uniform. Think about what happens in your living room and then approach its lighting by concentrating on specific areas of interest.

In the room on the right, wall sconces bounce indirect light off the ceiling. Traditional table lamps make adequate reading lights, while small portable floor lights, using miniature R 20 lamps, can be precisely directed. Behind the louvre window shades incandescent strip lights simulate sunlight.

In the elegant room below, low-voltage accent lights are used to highlight the various objects displayed on the mantelpiece. Further low-voltage fixtures above the sofa illuminate both the books and the art. They are balanced by table lamps, with large openings top and bottom.

Lighting art Many living areas contain works of art. If you choose, these can be a focal point of the room. Many works on a large wall are best served by the technique of wall washing (see page 105), which will evenly illuminate all the works displayed. You might like to highlight individual works using accent lights or framing projectors (see page 129). 'Picture' lights, directly attached to individual works, are an alternative choice. These lights are most practical for lighting pictures no taller than 610mm (2ft). Otherwise, light falls off so rapidly with distance that the bottom of many tall paintings ends up in the dark.

All colors deteriorate in ultraviolet light, but watercolors, pastels, and fabrics with natural dyes are especially susceptible to it. Keep these out of sunlight, and obtain an ultraviolet filter for artificial light.

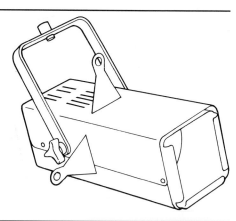

In the room on the right, most of the light comes from semi-recessed fixtures using silver bowl lamps in a parabolic reflector (see p. 128). These can be adjusted and focused to avoid glare, and here have been positioned to accent a picture and flowers. The light, monochrome surfaces provide enough bounced light for general illumination.

In the living room on the left, the metal balcony railing on the right-hand side has been put to much the same use as metal pipes in the theatre – theatrical spotlights have been fixed to it. These lights are portable and are plugged into sockets located along the metal balcony rail. The beam of the high-wattage lamps can be shaped into almost any form by use of the shutters, and the edge of the beam may be sharp- or soft-focused by moving the lens train (see lamp detail, above left).

There are ten different lighting circuits in the room on the right, all of which are controlled by dimmers. The brick wall on the left is lit by low-voltage spots concealed in a small bay. At the for end of the wall, a spread lens diffuses vertical streaks of light downwards, accentuating the wall's texture. The angle of the spread lens has been adjusted 90° to spread the light horizontally and cast an even wash of light on the painting in the foreground.

Cleverly used 'signal' lights are recessed into the round stairwell. All the other light in the room comes from low-voltage adjustable spotlights.

As a general rule, strong directional light should strike your paintings at an angle of 60° from horizontal. If you are looking straight ahead of you at the picture, this angle is a good compromise: it avoids both shadows from frames and reflections from protective glass or varnished finishes. But think about your normal sitting positions as well, so you are not subjected to glare from these same shiny surfaces when seated.

Sculpture and other three-dimensional objects – for instance, a vase on an end table – should be lit by fixtures with an adjustable focus. A general rule is to try and maintain contrast ratios of 6:1 (see page 20). Higher levels tend to obscure detail in the shadowed area and lower levels may 'flatten' the three-dimensionality.

Lighting plants The uplighting of large plants is a common way of introducing an area of luminal interest into a room. Most types of fixtures use directional display lamps that cause distinct shadows on your ceiling – which you may or may not like. Fixtures using A lamps, or display lamps fitted with a diffusing glass, create shadows that are less harsh. Certain plants have heat-sensitive areas on the underside of their leaves and you should avoid directing strong uplights at them.

Concealed lighting A fireplace is often a living room's focal point and, if you light the objects on your mantelpiece, this will serve to concentrate attention on the area, with or without a roaring fire.

Valances and coves are good places in which to hide cold cathode, fluorescent, or incandescent lamps.

For maximum dispersion, the lamp should be as close to the opening as possible while remaining out of sight line. Using this technique to bounce light off a pale ceiling provides a soft, indirect *ambiance*. And if the ceiling is peaked, arched, or otherwise not flat, architectural interest is added.

Concealed lighting behind architectural features is not appropriate for lighting art, but you may enjoy its wall-grazing quality. Recessing light in niches and window wells can also add dimensional interest to your space.

Using portable fixtures Many living rooms, especially those with a period flavor, employ floor-standing or table fixtures almost exclusively. If most of your lighting plugs into sockets, there are a few things to bear in mind. Try not to run cable to wall sockets across the areas where people walk, and running them under rugs can be a fire hazard. After all, sockets can always be fitted into your floor.

Depending on whether the fixture is for atmospheric or task light, you should consider the size of the shade's opening, both top and bottom, as this controls the spread of the light (see page 120). You need to be aware of the brightness of the shade itself. If it is too bright it will be glaring, especially if viewed against dark walls. Almost all floor or table lamps can have an in-line dimmer attached to their cable (see pages 130–31).

Task lighting If specific detailed or prolonged tasks are often done in your living room, you need to provide light specifically designed for the task (see page 62).

Cutting holes in mirrors is tricky but very effective. In the symbolic Spring Room from Charles Jencks' Thematic House on the right, two semi-recessed adjustable spotlights have been set into ceiling mirrors. Used to highlight the busts above the mantelpiece, their cool light contrasts strikingly with the other light in the room.

The capital of the column on the left has glass and lighting built into it, and this provides the room with soft, atmospheric light, augmented by a traditional small table fixture. The warm light of the capital and table lamp blends easily with the firelight, while the statues above stand out, accentuated by the cooler light of the accent spots.

D·I·N·I·N·G R·O·O·M·S

Your dining room may be a self-contained room, it may be part of your living room, or it may be part of your kitchen. You may use it every day, every weekend, or only for dinner parties. Your dining room may also be your library, your study, your home office, your playroom – or it may just be for dining. How elaborately you light it depends on how you use it, as well as on your budget and your personal taste.

Whatever function your particular dining room fulfils, your main goal in lighting it is to create an atmosphere comfortable to dine in. In theory, areas where carving and serving occur need to be thought of as work surfaces and lit accordingly (see page 132 for appropriate levels). This would include the table and perhaps a serving counter or sideboard. But in practice, lighting in these areas tends to be approached aesthetically.

Directional downlighting Lighting for the table is usually in the form of an overhead fixture that adequately covers the area. (If your table expands you should consider two lighting circuits, one for the center and another one for the two ends.) Directional downlights over the table area will enhance the table settings by producing many reflective highlights. But although good for the table, downlights mean that the people around it are seen in deep, steep shadows – which are quite unflattering. Dimming the light enhances faces – but then you lose the highlights on the table.

The oldest remedy in the world is to add candlelight. Placed along the center of the table, it provides the soft warm fill light that makes everyone look better, while also adding additional sparkle to nearby glossy surfaces. In any case, humans are phototropic beings – we are attracted to light. The single candle between two people is uniquely attracting.

If your table is very reflective – with a glass, polished marble, or lacquer surface – directional downlights may cause annoying reflections. Certainly angling this type of light inevitably bounces light into someone's eyes. You might also need to consider color reflection – a bright green tablecloth will influence the color of the light reflected back to people's faces and other surfaces.

Pendant fixtures A shaded pendant fixture hung over the table is often used in dining rooms. This type of fitting throws light up to the ceiling and transmits some diffuse light through the shade. Most of the light is still directed downwards, so the lamp should be shielded from

Five pendant lamps over the table serve to define the dining area in what is otherwise a flexible space. Their small size and their height above the table ensure that they will not obstruct the view of any dinner guest. However, the bare lamp protruding beyond the fixture's aperture can easily be a source of glare.

direct view and sufficiently diffused to prevent any glare. To eliminate glare, you may find you are hanging your pendant so low that you cannot see the person opposite. Many pendants now are available with height-adjusting mechanisms, so the answer may be to move the pendant a little higher and dim the lamp.

Chandeliers A beautiful source of sparkle, traditional chandeliers are most successful when many small low-wattage lamps are used. These create lots of highlights and atmosphere, but not much useful illumination. Using brighter lamps does not help; their glare just overpowers the sparkle they should create.

Fill lighting To enhance the space as well as the occupants, rooms dominated by chandeliers need other light sources. Those that contribute a soft indirect light are said to provide 'fill' light. This could be from candles, or concealed perimeter lighting in coves and behind valances or from wall sconces. Opaque wall brackets direct all their light upward, bouncing indirect light off the ceiling, while those with translucent glass direct some diffused light out the side, not unlike windows. With glass sconces the walls should not be too dark, lest the contrast between lighted glass and wall be excessive. Floor sitting uplights and torcheres also provide good indirect fill lighting.

In addition to all the soft fill light any room benefits from fixtures which accent salient features.

The dining area on the far left is lit by a single surface-mounted fixture over the center of the table. This unusual fixture consists of lenses and mirrors that can redistribute light from a single central source in any direction. Here, some of the light is directed down on to the place settings, and some is directed out at the wall.

In addition, a circle of cold cathode has been fitted around the perimeter of the ceiling dome, where its soft glow accentuates the dome shape. There are further lighting units behind the window valance.

In the stylish dining room on the left, recessed downlights provide the main lighting for the table and give the glass its sparkle. Candlelight softens any harsh shadows caused by the over-head light. The track system running around the room's perimeter is equipped with a linear halogen fixture, to wash large areas, and a spotlight fixture to highlight the bust.

Because of structural difficulties with the ceiling of the room on the left, a special box was fitted, housing a number of PAR 38 lamps. These can be focused in any direction: some are used to highlight walls, others are employed to accent paintings, while several, of course, light the dining area itself. For maximum control, the lamps could be individually circuited.

K·I·T·C·H·E·N·S

In many parts of the world family life centers around the kitchen. If this is true of your house, the atmosphere in your kitchen should be conducive to more than just work. And even if your kitchen *is* only for cooking, those who cook spend as many hours in the kitchen as in any other room. For that reason alone your kitchen should be enjoyable to work in.

FUNCTIONAL —LIGHTING—

The main function of kitchen lighting is to help you in the task of food preparation. Since this involves sharp implements and a moderate degree of speed and accuracy, the kitchen should be supplied with plenty of comfortable light.

There are three task areas in a kitchen: the cooker (or range), the sink, and the preparation counters. These surfaces should be treated in the same way as any other task area (see Workrooms, page 62, for more information about task lighting).

Under-cabinet lighting The local lighting for tasks usually comes from under a kitchen cabinet or shelf. If the work surface is long, fluorescent tubes are an excellent choice. They provide a high volume of lumens (see page 77), their shadow quality is soft, and their color rendering is now comparable with incandescent light.

The comfortable, well-planned kitchen on the right is lit by several hanging lamps with metal shades. Holding ordinary A lamps, they cast a wide beam of warm light, both practical and intimate.

In addition, the butcher's block in the foreground is lit with a semi-recessed adjustable display spotlight (not visible in the photograph).

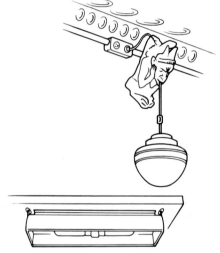

The unpretentious kitchen on the left employs several different light sources. Over the main work counter on the right-hand side, several PAR 38s are mounted on a track. Six lamps are necessary to light the work surface evenly with such fixtures. The other work surface has been lit by antique theatrical footlights, taking linear incandescent lamps (see detail, above).

The fitting over the sink was a collage of found parts (see detail, above right), and includes a two-position switch – bright for washing up, and dim for a more atmospheric light.

Kitchen surfaces are frequently more reflective than those elsewhere in the house. Water-resistant surfaces like stainless steel, tiles, porcelain, and laminates will reflect more light than wood, so under-cabinet lighting must be planned to minimize glaring reflections. This usually entails placing the lamps towards the front of the shelf or cabinet.

Under-cabinet-mounted appliances are now becoming more widely available – if they really catch on the traditional way of lighting work surfaces may have to be rethought. Perhaps appliance manufacturers will add lights to the underside of their coffee makers and microwaves.

Whatever under-cabinet lighting you use should be shielded from direct view, both when you are standing and when you are seated.

Ceiling lighting If you do not have under-shelf or under-cabinet lighting, then your work surfaces will be lit from the ceiling. In this case the illumination should be placed near the edge of the counter surface, so that neither you nor the wall-hung cabinets cast shadows on the work surfaces. Fixtures that provide a wide coverage of soft-edged light are preferable – such as linear halogen, A, and fluorescent (see pages 78–93). There are numerous fittings – either recessed, surface- or pendant-mounted (see pages 100–25) that fulfil these requirements. Your choice will be dictated by the design of your kitchen.

If you do light work surfaces with display lamps (see pages 82–83), you will probably need more than you anticipate to cover the surface evenly.

Lighting for the above kitchen demonstrates how available bits and pieces can be used creatively to construct lamps. Essentially the fixtures are nothing more than lampholders with R lamps, some of which are directed at the work surface, while others are directed at the ceiling for an indirect light. Traditional under-cabinet task lighting has been built into the storage cabinets, for extra light where it is most needed.

Three different light sources fulfil a variety of purposes in the kitchen above. Fixtures taking A lamps have been built into the pot rack that hangs over the center island. Surface-mounted fixtures above the stove pick out the cooking area, while recessed units throw light down to the carpet, an unusual flooring choice.

Adjusting the levels of these light sources, all separately circuited on dimmers, allows the owner to make the kitchen interesting when viewed from the living room.

You will probably also need a general 'fill' source of lighting to reduce shadows and balance the contrast of these directional lamps.

Storage Storage cabinets are the other main candidate for illumination in the kitchen. Most of the time you settle for reflected light from work surfaces to allow you to see your stored dishes, foods, and utensils. However, if most of your work light is positioned low (under cabinets or shelves), you may need a general ceiling-mounted source or something that is specifically focused towards cabinet shelves. Additionally, a general lighting source may be needed to prevent excessive contrast between task and surrounding room.

——MOOD LIGHTING——

As work places, kitchens are frequently lit with high general levels of illumination. While appropriate for the immediate tasks at hand, this does not create the right atmosphere for relaxation. And since so much non-task time tends to be spent in the kitchen – especially if you eat in it at all – you should give special thought to a second lighting circuit that is separately controlled and intended to make your kitchen an interesting space to be in or look at.

Being able to control the lighting for each task area separately is a good idea. For much of the time you spend in it the kitchen is in daylight and, depending on the amount yours receives, you may only need to augment – for instance – one area at breakfast and a different area around lunch time. If that is the case, those

The simple, clean lines of the kitchen above are emulated by the equally simple and effective lighting system. Four recessed downlights provide general illumination for the entire kitchen, while under-cabinet lights give high-level lighting specifically for the work surfaces. In addition, the light that is reflecting off all the surfaces, even the glossy floor, helps to give this kitchen its feeling of extreme brightness and airiness.

areas might be on a separate circuit and have 'cooler' fluorescent sources, which will blend better with the color of daylight than 'warmer' incandescent ones.

When creating the alternative mood for your kitchen, you may find that simply leaving on the light above the stove top provides an appropriate mood for your needs. But, if this light is fluorescent or some other linear source, it may be too flat and dull, as well as often too bright on its own. If general lighting for the kitchen has been from around the perimeter, being able to dim that creates both a warm glow on the ceiling and a soft general *ambiance*.

Eating in the kitchen If your kitchen contains a dining area (or is in view of one), you probably want to distinguish between the kitchen as a work area and the kitchen as an eating area. In any case, for visual relief at the dining table you want another area of luminal interest.

Take advantage of the reflective surfaces found in most kitchens – often an interesting starting-point for creating a relaxed drama. Directional lighting creates attractive sparkle on glossy surfaces, which will vary with your viewing position. A few well-aimed 'spots' bounced off a tiled counter could supply the interest you want. If your cooking tools are on open display, you could treat them as sculpture and light them accordingly. Alternatively, perhaps directional lights aimed at your storage cabinets, when dimmed, will provide enough variety.

Lighting was considered at a very early stage of the planning for the Indian Summer kitchen below, from Charles Jencks' symbolic Thematic House. Fixtures using A lamps have been recessed into shelves, giving a wide distribution of light.

Normally, placing such fixtures as close to the wall as they are here would produce distracting scallops of light; in this kitchen, the scallops are images in reverse of the capitals on top of the columns. Thus they enhance the architectural features of the kitchen, as well as providing plenty of practical work light.

B·E·D·R·O·O·M·S

Before you plan your bedroom lighting, you need to ask yourself searching questions about the way you use the room – bedrooms can be used in such a variety of ways.

If your bedroom is more for fantasy than practical living, you may want to concentrate on creating appropriate moods and *ambiance*. You can combine functional and mood lighting in one room, but rarely in the same light sources.

FUNCTIONAL LIGHTING

Begin by asking yourself some practical questions: Do you read in bed? Is there a study area or a lounge area in the room? Is there a full-length mirror for dressing? Where is the wardrobe? Does it receive adequate reflected light or does it need specific illumination? Do you have a make-up table? The complexity of tasks and uses should be reflected in the way the bedroom is lit.

Reading lights If you like to read in bed, a good task light is a must. This fixture should obviously be placed near you as you read. It should be out of your way when you are sitting, yet the light must not shine in your eyes when you are lying down. And its arm should not jut out so far that the light is focused back at you. Your reading light should also be flexible, so that as you shift your position you can eliminate glare from glossy pages.

If you share your bed, and one of you reads while the other sleeps, the reading lamps should be put near the center line of the bed, so that the fixtures can be focused outwards, or away from the person trying to sleep. Lamps on bedside tables do not usually make good reading lights since, if their general light is strong enough for reading, it also illuminates most of the room.

Mirror lighting A full-length mirror is one that demands proper lighting – of you, not it. A narrow area of light large enough to illuminate your whole figure at the distance from the mirror where you normally stand should be adequate. A 45° angle is flattering.

Overhead lighting of this sort is especially suitable if you are dressing for artificial light. The color of daylight is different, as is its direction; if you are dressing for daylight, consider using a length of daylight-balanced fluorescent tubes around your mirror.

Wardrobes and closets Wardrobe lighting is usually overlooked – yet nothing is more frustrating than having to turn on all the lights in the room, hoping that enough will be reflected into the wardrobe to let you find the shoes that you haven't seen for three weeks.

The easiest way to light a wardrobe is with an A lamp or a fluorescent tube. The lamp should be positioned just inside the wardrobe, close to the door, so that the light can get into shelf areas as well as illuminate hanging clothing. A simple lamp-holder with minimum shielding will

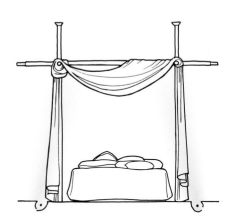

Gauzy material draped over portable photography poles creates an instant four-poster bed in the room on the right. Linear halogen lights with a broad distribution have been set into the floor (see detail, above). A string of Christmas-tree lights along the top of the bed adds to the playful feel. The Tizio lamp at the head of the bed is being used as a reading light.

If two of you share a bed, you should have a reading light each, as below. These lights should be adjustable, so that one of you can read while the other sleeps.

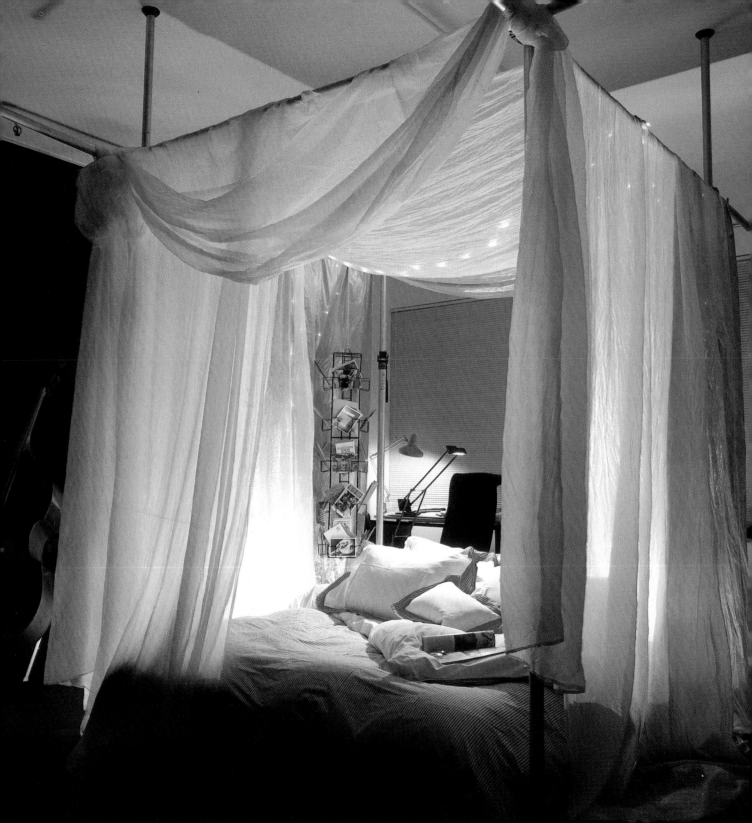

usually work. If you use an essentially bare lamp, make sure that it is not in danger of being easily broken. If you store your shoes under hanging clothing, you might consider a step light mounted low in the wall (see page 127). Wardrobe lights can be activated by small door switches or by a simple pull chain.

Controlling your lights You should give some thought to the control of your bedroom lights. If the controls are installed around your bed, you will find it more convenient for midnight excursions to the bathroom, or indeed for setting up mood lighting (see below) without running all over the room adjusting switches and dimmers. Three-way switching/dimming is advisable all the same, so that you can turn lights on from the door upon entering the room – for safety – and off from bed before retiring – for convenience.

MOOD LIGHTING

Apart from your practical lighting needs, dictated by the size and multi-use of your bedroom, some lighting elements should be there to add decorative and aesthetic interest to your bedroom space. If your space has many uses and there are multiple lighting circuits, the control of these may be enough. If the space is small, however, and mainly used for sleeping, you should consider additional decorative lighting, chosen depending on your budget and how much time you spend in the room.

The bedroom on the left, designed by John Wright, includes a small study area, with a mirrored wall helping to give a sense of expanded space. The lighting has been carefully thought out, with each specific need separately catered for.

A reading light is mounted out of sight directly over the head of the bed; a semi-recessed adjustable spotlight is lighting the photographs on the wall; a downlight holding an A lamp defines the area around the desk; and a table-top task light is used as the source of illumination for work.

The low ceilings of the attic bedroom below enable small, unobtrusive table lamps to be effective as sources of indirect light bounced off the ceiling. Further light comes from recessed lights placed in the deeply recessed alcoves. The pendant chandelier, visible in the mirror, adds a little extra luminal and visual interest.

C·H·I·L·D·R·E·N'S R·O·O·M·S

Children seem to outgrow their rooms as fast as they do their clothes. Unlike clothing, lighting can help make a room flexible, so that it expands with the growing needs of the child.

To light your child's room effectively, again ask yourself a few questions. How do you anticipate the room changing – from, say, a nursery to the private domain of a teenager? Will the cot eventually be replaced by a bed or by a desk? Is the room primarily for sleeping and, later, homework? Or is it also the playroom, crammed with toys?

Needs of the nursery In a young child's room or nursery, safety is the main consideration. Lamps and fixtures – particularly portable and clip-on ones – should be placed out of a child's reach. Quite apart from their electrical dangers, they build up heat. Such fixtures are also in danger of being knocked over and broken. You might also consider covering open plug sockets with 'dummy' covers, so your child cannot stick anything into the holes.

Young children often prefer to have some light while they are going to sleep. You could use an overhead light on a dimmer. A dimmed light is a great advantage with young children; it enables you to attend to a child in the night without having to turn on unpleasantly bright light. You can buy small plug-in night lights, while moulded plastic fittings in the shapes of various animals are also available (see page 55). These are

lit from inside and make delightful night lights. But, if you fall for one of these, remember that the more attractive the appearance of the light, the more likely your child is to try and get hold of it – with possibly disastrous consequences. Make sure that all electrical components are shielded and out of the child's reach.

Needs of the older child By the time a child can read, he or she has usually learned a little about the dangers of electricity – or at least he knows that lamps and fixtures get hot and need to be treated with care. This is the stage when a portable or clip-on reading lamp for bed becomes a possible option. Position this type of lamp so that it does not get in the way of the child's other play activities – especially important if you are dealing with bunk beds.

If two children sharing a room do sleep in bunk beds, the child in the lower bunk may lose out if the general source of illumination is ceiling-mounted. Or the child in the lower bunk may get a reading light, while the child above is expected to make do with the general light, which is often not suitable or adequate. Both children need their own bedside lights, which should be positioned to one side of the bedhead out of the way.

——TRACK LIGHTING——

A good choice for a child's room, track lighting can be adapted to the changing needs of the child. A 'cross' or rectangle pattern usually ensures

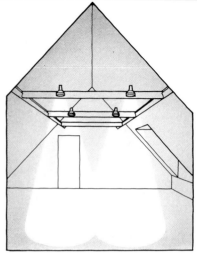

The spacious attic playroom on the right has lines of track recessed into the horizontal beams. Each track is separately controlled, which means that any point in the room can be emphasized by light. In addition, the track fixtures are flexible, so that the light can be focused over the beams, directed down to the floor for specific tasks (as shown in the detail, above), or aimed at the ceiling for indirect bounced light. This lighting system will adapt easily to the changing needs of the children as they grow up.

that the light can reach the places where it will eventually be needed.

In the early stages, when the room is still largely a nursery, general illumination of a soft and diffuse quality is pleasing: it gives a bright, open feeling to the room, especially if the nursery does not receive a lot of natural daylight. You could use A lamp fixtures with a wide distribution pattern (see page 101); alternatively, you could direct the light to walls and/or ceiling, giving indirect illumination. At this stage the only extra light you may need – apart from perhaps a night light – is a task light focused on the changing and storage areas.

As the room evolves into a play area, you will want a higher level of lighting. General overall lighting is still called for – the play area always seems to encompass the whole of the space. But other fixtures can easily be added to the track and directed where needed.

The installation of a multi-circuit track pays dividends when the child – or two children sharing – reaches the stage of wanting to exert some control over the environment. If a first circuit is used to provide general light, the second circuit can be made up of more specific display fittings. These could accent posters, a collection of 'things' – they are a way of shaping the environment so that the child feels it is truly his or hers. Having these circuits on a dimmer provides additional control.

The homework or desk area is most easily lit with a traditional task lamp that focuses on the work surface (see Workrooms, page 62, for more about task lights).

An extended section of track runs along the length of this children's room, shown both above and right. Because the room is narrow, central overhead track allows light to reach almost any part of it without glare becoming a problem.

The only point in the room that cannot be reached by the track is the study area on the right, because it has been tucked underneath a bunk bed to save space. A classic architect's lamp has therefore been installed as the task light for the desk.

Various brightly colored, fanciful lamps have been designed with children specifically in mind. They can be either wall-mounted or free-standing; a selection is illustrated on the left.

If you add a dimmer to this type of lamp, it can make a most successful and convenient nightlight in a nursery or young child's room.

The lighting in the room on the right has been designed to give its teenaged occupant maximum control. The central recessed fitting has a fresnel lens (see p. 129) and is by itself capable of supplying general illumination for the whole room.

The light directly above the head of the bed is used as a reading lamp, while the one next to it is easily adjusted to focus on whatever the room's owner wishes. At the desk an architect's fixture serves as the work light.

There is also a set of incandescent strip lights above the desk/wardrobe area; not turned on in this photograph, these can flush the ceiling with an extra, atmospheric glow.

B·A·T·H·R·O·O·M·S

The bathroom is usually the first place you confront yourself each morning and often the last place you see yourself each night. Ideally these moments of truth should occur in a well-designed space, where the light that first reveals you and that last sees you is appropriately complimentary to your features.

The scope of modern bathroom equipment is staggering. In addition to the obligatory sink, lavatory, and bath, you can have a separate shower, a bidet, a steam cabinet, a sauna, a jacuzzi, a lounging area, a dressing area, a sunbed, a hothouse, and almost anything else you want.

But, like the kitchen, notwithstanding all its possible auxiliary purposes, the bathroom remains primarily a task-oriented area. All bathrooms, whether they are tiny, private affairs or capable of handling a good sized party, have one thing in common: a task-oriented mirror, usually over the sink or the area into which the sink is set.

Mirror lighting Lighting this area effectively is the most important part of lighting your bathroom. Your routine critical analyses of yourself should be carried out in light that is objective yet complimentary, direct yet soft and shadowless, revealing yet nevertheless kind.

The best light for self-scrutiny is soft and straight on. The most suitable fixture is a copy or variation of the traditional theatrical make-up light. The fixture is a linear light source and can consist of many small low-wattage diffuse lamps or of long incandescent tubes. Ideally these 'strip' lights shoud surround the mirror on four sides; at the very least they should be on both sides of the mirror and mounted far enough apart so as not to be glaring at your normal viewing distance. Remember that many dim lamps make a more effective, less glaring strip light than two or three more intense lamps, which can be irritatingly dazzling.

Actors often add colors to their lights to imitate stage lighting. Since daylight, office lighting (usually cool white fluorescent), and incandescent domestic lighting are all very different in color, why should the area where you dress and/or make up not reflect these differences? You could have your mirror lighting on two separately controlled circuits, one in-

The room on the left contains a large jacuzzi, which can hold seven people. The low-voltage recessed lights in the background have deliberately been positioned very close to the wall, so their scallops of light provide visual interest as well as illuminating the bench that people sit on before or after entering the bath.

There is in addition a single, narrow, low-voltage spotlight placed directly above the tub for use when a more intimate atmosphere is wanted.

The linear design of the bathroom on the right is accentuated by the two lines of light built into the wall cavities and the long, illuminated ceiling. The two lines of light have been achieved by placing linear fluorescent lamps end to end (see detail, above). While they directly highlight the architecture, they indirectly light the user by bouncing light off the ceiling and sink counter.

The even illumination of the ceiling has been achieved by spacing fluorescent tubes the same distance from each other as from the opal acrylic that diffuses the light. The combination of diffused ceiling illumination with indirect, bounced light creates a softly shadowed and flattering atmosphere.

candescent and one fluorescent (of 4000 Kelvin with a good Color Rendering Index – see page 91). You could then use the circuits independently or in conjunction, according to what light you were about to be seen in.

Additional bathroom lighting
Lighting resources and the technology now available are equal to the most complex bathroom arrangements. How sumptuously you light your bathroom will be in direct proportion to its decorative appointments and your personal lifestyle. Do you spend as little time in the room as possible, going through your tasks quickly? Or do you enjoy luxuriating in the bathroom, seeing it as a pleasant place to relax? Do you read in the bath? Do you shave in the shower? All specific tasks that take place in your bathroom deserve to have lighting considered for them. Think carefully, and then decide what lighting to install.

Observing local regulations The functional nature of the bathroom places some limitation on the light fixtures you can use. Many countries have regulations restricting lighting in wet areas, for as everyone knows electricity and water do not mix. In Britain switches must take the inelegant form of pull-cords, while in most states they must be located outside of the bathroom. Electrical outlets, for shavers or hair driers, require a specially earthed socket, one with a built-in extremely sensitive circuit-breaker.

Certainly, all wet areas like showers and baths should be supplied with watertight housings. And the high moisture levels in bathrooms almost invariably demand fixtures that have at least been approved for damp locations. Unfortunately most manufacturers have a limited, even dull, standard range of watertight fixtures. But there are ways around this – try investigating catalogues produced by makers of commercial fixtures, or those from manufacturers designing fixtures for use out of doors or underwater.

In the bathroom pictured below, the two strips of lights on either side of the mirror provide enough light for the entire room. As well as casting good general light they are, of course, also effective make-up lights. The mirror is wide and the strip lights far enough apart, so the person looking in the mirror will not experience any visual discomfort as a result of glare.

Two PAR 38 downlights recessed into the ceiling are used for additional dramatic impact.

The mirror tiles and polished marble in the bathroom on the left are such highly reflective surfaces that they allow the four downlights in the ceiling to illuminate the entire room adequately. In the mirror a strip light is visible; composed of eight small frosted lamps, it functions as a soft light for applying make-up.

Notice how mirrors placed opposite each other give reflections that apparently extend to infinity.

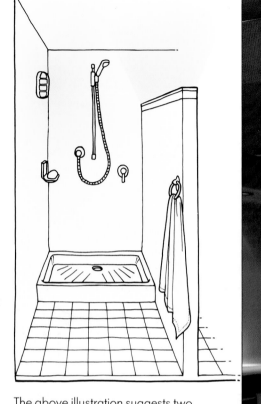

The above illustration suggests two possible alternative methods of lighting a shower. A fluorescent or linear incandescent fixture could be built into the partition wall with diffusing plastic; or, as shown on the opposite wall, a weatherproof surface-mounted fixture could be used.

There is a strong sense of drama in the bathroom on the left, created by the contrast of primary colors used for the shelving units and towels.

Low-voltage, surface-mounted and recessed accent lights reinforce the theatrical feel. This type of strong, intense and directional light – while dramatic – is not necessarily flattering; however, the designer deliberately sacrificed practical function for dramatic effect.

In many countries the lighting in the bathroom on the right would be illegal, and it is certainly not completely safe. Nonetheless; it demonstrates how much fun can be had with the imaginative use of lighting.

Striking, diagonal stripes of neon light complement the bright yellow of the water pipes and the mirror outline. On either side of the mirror, a circular fluorescent lamp provides the general light for the rest of the bathroom.

W·O·R·K·R·O·O·M·S

By definition, work spaces include all the parts of the house where specific tasks are performed. Some work spaces have already been discussed elsewhere in this section; apart from these, a workroom can be anywhere in the house. Yours may be a corner of the garage convertd to a wood-working shop, a laundry, utility, or sewing room, or perhaps a formidable private library.

—TASK LIGHTING—

How much lighting you need for your task depends on several factors: the size of the task (large objects are easier to see than small ones); the length of time spent at the task (the longer you spend the more light you need); your age (people in their sixties may need ten times more light than a twenty year old carrying out the same task).

If speed is important or if accuracy needs to be high, then generally you need more light still. Reading in your study does not make the same demands on time and accuracy as working with a power saw. The contrast of a book (black ink on white paper) is high, and predetermined, while with most other tasks the contrast level is variable. In general, the lower the contrast of the task, the more light you need – for instance, sewing a pale fabric with white thread is a low-contrast task wanting high light levels.

Shadow It is probably obvious that you should not work in shadow, either your own or anything else's.

Ideally the whole of your task plane should be evenly lit. Fluorescent tubes are a good choice for work surfaces; so are incandescent fittings that have diffusers or otherwise illuminate large areas. Additionally, the shadows caused by these sources are soft-edged, which means that your eyes find them less tiring than harsh, high-contrast shadows.

Reflection and glare Just as you do not want to work in your own shadow, you also want to avoid glare. In its least offensive form, glare will lower your contrast while, in its most disabling form, it will shine directly in your eyes (see page 17).

Reflections off a work surface can best be controlled by placing the light source to one side of your task. The angle to avoid is the one created by placing the source too far in front of yourself, causing reflected light to bounce back into your eyes. The compromise position is to shine your light source directly above the work surface or slightly behind yourself (but not so far as to cast your own shadow on your task).

Needs of desk work The classic task light, the architect's lamp, is still as useful as ever for small surfaces such as a desk. Architect's lamps are now available in designs to suit the most simple or the most elegant situations (see page 122). As in any work environment, you should control the contrast between the task area and the immediate surround in order to prevent eye fatigue. A ratio of 3:1 is recommended.

During the daytime, the attic workroom on the right is flooded with natural light entering through a skylight window. For night-time use, the owner of the flat has designed six, low-voltage, miniature fittings and placed them all along the edge of the wall and on the desk. They are used to provide precise illumination of the various different task surfaces.

The versatile light illustrated below is a fluorescent tube suspended from the ceiling. For indirect, diffused light it can be directed upwards; when direct task light is called for, it is simply inverted.

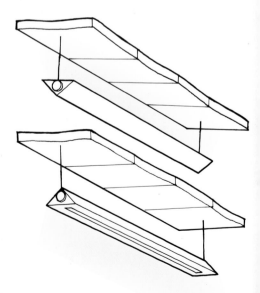

Needs of library work If your work space is a library, then you probably want to illuminate the bookshelves. This can best be accomplished by using the techniques of wall washing (see page 105) or undershelf lighting (see page 42).

Needs of garage work Lighting in a garage does not have to be elaborate, but you should still take trouble over the placement of the fixtures. Do not put a fixture over the center of a car, since this only illuminates the top, casting shadows across all the places you want to see. Instead place your lighting to the front and/or back of the car. (If you have a multi-car garage, place the fixtures between the cars.)

The fanciful study on the right uses a track lighting system suspended below the reinforcing joists of the ceiling. The track runs across the entire length of the room.

Fixtures holding silver bowl lamps with parabolic reflectors are used as accent lights for the many pale artefacts on the walls. The work light for the desk comes from an A lamp in a fixture with a wide-distribution reflector; this is positioned directly above the desk.

The room on the left has excellent work light. A luminous ceiling has been created by hiding several fluorescent lamps behind sheets of acrylic, and as a result there is a general high level of overall illumination, casting soft, gentle shadows.

Lengths of track on the ceiling above the work benches hold fixtures containing R lamps; these are easily adjustable, and their light can therefore be directed either towards storage areas or at specific tasks, according to individual preference.

The study below has such a low ceiling that exceptionally wide-angled fixtures were used to light it. The chosen fixture is adjustable, surface-mounted, with a large-diameter shade.

A silver bowl lamp reflects the light into the shade, which in turn bounces it on to the bookshelves and walls, producing a pleasant, wide distribution of even light.

O·N·E-R·O·O·M LI·V·I·N·G

The urban phenomenon of one-room living is a difficult problem, one that demands creative solutions.

Where to begin Work out the multiple uses you expect a single area to serve. For example, if your bed is a pull-out sofa that your guests sit on, then you should light it for both sitting and sleeping. As a bed it may only need a properly placed reading light. If you make this fixture flexible, by day it can be focused on your bedside table, which holds a flower arrangement, not an alarm clock.

The one table in your room is probably a desk as well as your eating surface. You might use a pendant-mounted linear fluorescent in a rotating tube. For work, the light is directed downwards, but when you eat you rotate the light towards the ceiling – perhaps placing a color filter on top of it to warm the color and lessen the intensity (see page 62).

Manipulating light Watever final solution you come up with, flexibility and control should be your guiding principles. Since the single space can be confining, the aim of most people is to make it appear the opposite, open and airy. You can do this with wall washing techniques, as a brighter wall will make the room appear wider. Bouncing light off the ceiling can make it appear higher, while providing plenty of indirect light for the room.

The flexibility of lighting can be a great ally. Separately controlled electrical circuits will help define specific areas. If each of these circuits is also on a dimmer, you can highlight one area while balancing others against it.

Many people who rent studio apartments do not expect to stay for long, and do not want to invest in permanently installed lighting. Track lighting can easily move with you, and the extra cost of multi-circuit track is well worth it. One circuit could hold fixtures that provide a general light and another could be for fixtures throwing accent light to various parts of the room.

Being less adaptable, table lamps can be limiting; while a floor lamp with a flexible head can be adjusted upwards for atmospheric bounce light or downwards as a reading light. Wall-mounted fixtures can be effective and, if chosen carefully, can live to see another home. It is up to you to decide whether you want a general widespread light (say, from a linear halogen fixture) or a sharp intense accent light (from a low-voltage spot). In either case, buying an adjustable fixture is worthwhile.

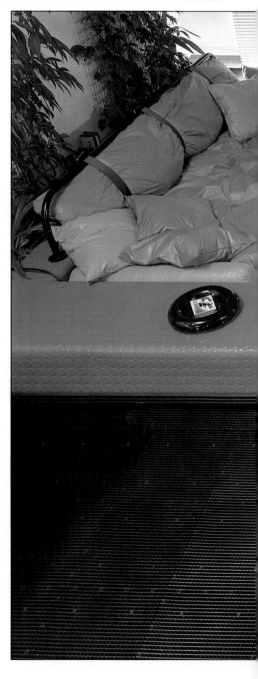

The main light source, in the studio apartment on the right, comes from four easily portable inspection lamps, fitted with low-wattage A lamps.

Apart from these, a halogen floor light (see **4**, p. 124) provides a cooler light; and the owner also makes good use of a number of miniature clip-on spotlights. By day these are attached to the vertical Venetian blinds; at bedtime, the same lights clip on to the rails behind the long sofa cushions (which are actually duvets) and make excellent bedside lights.

C·O·N·S·E·R·V·A·T·O·R·I·E·S

There are many different kinds of conservatory, but almost all present the same lighting problems. At night glass becomes a mirror-like reflector. Any unshielded lamp will be reflected in one or all surfaces, depending on your position in the room. If the lamp is intense, the reflection will be glaring. Even a soft light will be very bright against the blackness of the glass, and so will its reflection.

Problems with reflection Any directional spotlights must be well shielded and their position in relation to the most frequent viewing angle needs careful planning. Generally, a single pendant fixture is unsuccessful, because at a comfortable intensity it will hardly produce any useful illumination at all.

As in any darkly colored room (and at night glass is black), many low-level lamps are less annoying than a few bright ones. This is especially true of glass, where the reflection of many dim sources is more likely to be seen as sparkle than glare. There are numerous 'strings' of tiny low-voltage lamps available that could be used, for example, to outline the shape of the roof (see page 127).

Electrical difficulties A large percentage of add-on conservatories are built from kits, which often do not allow for wiring within the strips that support the glass. It is thus important to confer with your contractor and/or electrician about how to make your proposed lighting work. Many low-voltage strips, for instance, have self-adhesive backings.

If your conservatory juts out into your lit garden, you will need to consider the balance of the two areas. With carefully controlled reflections and harmonious light levels, the two spaces can be made to appear almost as one. Too much light inside and too many reflections will make it difficult to see beyond the glass to the garden. The brighter the outside lighting is, the less the glass acts as a mirror from the inside of the house.

If getting electricity to your conservatory is impossible, and you have a glass roof, you might consider lighting it from above by using weatherproof fixtures attached to the outside of the building. There is nothing to prevent you from doing this anyway, except perhaps budget.

The conservatory on the right extends the height of two floors. Three low-voltage spotlights are fitted on the wall of the upper floor. Of these, one is directed at the angel, while the other two light the plants from above.

In addition, five portable low-voltage spotlights (see detail below) on the floor run around the perimeter of the room. As well as accenting the plants from underneath, these spots cast shadows on the ceiling — a little extra visual stimulus for the owner sitting in the study on the upper level.

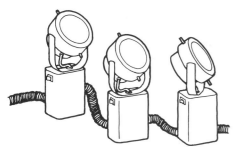

Standing lamps and wall sconces that cast their light upward are the main source of light for the conservatory on the left. To prevent the black, mirror-like glass from making the lights appear excessively bright and dazzling, the lamps have, of course, been put on dimmers.

As this conservatory is used for dining, appropriately candlelight has been added. By throwing light on to people's faces, it softens the shadows and creates a mood of intimacy.

E·XT·E·R·I·O·R·S & G·A·R·D·E·N·S

Illuminating the outside of your home serves two functions: first, to keep it secure and, second, to enhance its character. Lighting for one does not necessarily give you the other.

—SECURITY LIGHTING—

There seem to be two schools of thought about security lighting.

Floodlighting your grounds One option is to maintain a more or less general floodlighting of your grounds and points of entry, such as windows and doors. The theory is that observant neighbors will easily be able to see any stranger snooping about your property. If you decide to opt for this, the relatively new HID lamps are almost ideal (see page 94): they are long-lasting, require little maintenance, and give high lumens per watt (see page 77). This makes them less expensive to operate than incandescent lamps. Many pole-type fixtures using HID lamps give a wide dispersion of light.

There is one problem with HID lamps: they are extremely bright. One lamp could illuminate the whole façade and front yard of a house. But a single bright element in an otherwise darkened and tranquil neighborhood is an annoying source of glare. Also, a single intense light source is less flattering to your home than several less bright ones.

So, if you do decide to adopt this system, position or shield your fixtures so that light does not inadver-

Square outdoor fixtures have been placed beneath the gutter drains outside the house on the left. Reflecting the geometric shape of the house, these fixtures use PAR 38 lamps and throw a good deal of light around the immediate vicinity.

The grazing quality of the light also serves to emphasize the texture and materials used to construct the exterior walls.

The small selection of outdoor fixtures illustrated on the right is not intended to be representative of the range of choice available. The fixtures shown are intended simply to give an idea of some of the possible approaches to garden lighting. Light can come from ground level, from a tree or wall, from the top of a building, or even from your swimming pool.

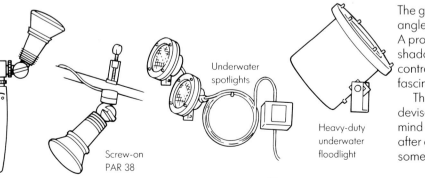

Double
PAR 38
on spike

Screw-on
PAR 38

Underwater
spotlights

Heavy-duty
underwater
floodlight

The garden above is lit by many low-angle lights placed near ground level. A profusion of bright light and dark shadow creates a series of extreme contrasts, which make the garden fascinating to view from indoors.

The lighting has indeed been devised with the view from inside in mind – someone sitting in the garden after dark might find the lights somewhat harsh and glaring.

tently stray into the street or extend to your neighbor's property.

Light only when it's needed The second school of security lighting assumes that your neighbors are not constantly observing your home for you, but need to be prompted. In this case an alarm system is connected to your exterior lighting. When a window or door is tampered with, an alarm signal activates the exterior lighting – if you wish it, the same signal could also set off your indoor lighting and an audible alarm. You could even arrange it so that your lights flash on and off, thereby frightening away most burglars, as well as attracting the attention of your neighbors. This school of thought further reasons that if your doors and windows are not well illuminated, a potential thief would need a flash light to see, and the moving light would attract attention.

While the second alarm system initially costs more to install than the first, it does preclude your burning lamps constantly, so letting you concentrate on lighting your exterior more for home and garden enhancement than for security.

ENHANCEMENT — LIGHTING —

The eye adapts to very low levels of light and your vision feels comfortable. This is called 'scotopic' vision. While you see in the 'dark', your color perception is poor.

Exterior lighting links your indoor space with your out-of-door area. Since your eye, once adapted, functions very well with little light, low levels of illumination are usually ad-

equate out of doors. And, as mentioned earlier, any bright unshielded light source is glaring in the dark.

Exterior fixtures How much effort and money you want to put into your exterior lighting depends on how much time you spend out of doors at night as well as on your budget. There are many beautiful and functional fixtures available (see pages 126–27). These are made of high-grade materials to resist corrosion and are sealed against the elements. They are therefore expensive. Depending on local regulations, exterior wiring can also be more expensive than the same wiring indoors. Add to this the fact that many dimmer sources are more pleasing than a few very bright ones, and you will see that the cost can quickly mount up.

Surprisingly little light was necessary to make the bold statement above, where white walls are etched against a pitch-black sky. Only a few lights are being used: on the right-hand side, high on the wall, one lamp is lighting the statue; on the left-hand side, light emanates from a fixture placed low down near the stairway. The resulting shadows reveal the many different architectural forms of the buildings.

The lighting for the secluded roof garden on the right is provided by flexible fixtures holding PAR 38 lamps, which have been placed at intervals along the top of the walls.

Since all the plants are grown in tubs, it is possible to move them as well as to adjust the lights. In this way the owner can concentrate light on whichever textures, colors, flowers, or foliages are the most exciting at any given season of the year.

A good many outdoor fixtures are made to accept the new, energy-efficient compact fluorescent lamps, mostly the neat PL types (see page 93). However, most fixtures that use an A lamp could just as well use an SL lamp. As these compact sources are not yet dimmable, you should consider the brightness of the fixtures and choose the lowest adequate wattage.

Lighting the house Apart from the entranceway to your house (see page 26), there may be some architectural features worth illuminating. If, in the initial construction, lighting was not considered – that is, built into overhanging eaves or mounted on exterior walls – it is easiest to add lighting that is mounted in the grounds. (The drawback to this is that low angles are unnatural and distorting, tending to make homes look like national monuments.)

Lighting the garden It is often more flattering to light the garden or land around a house than it is to light the house itself. You can make the garden lighting exciting and elaborate, or you might simply confine it to a barbecue or patio area.

Fixtures are made to be placed almost anywhere: in the trees, on property-dividing walls, on buildings, on the ground, in the ground, underground. As long as you avoid glare, outdoor lighting can be as creative as your imagination wishes. Plants, shrubs, and trees look more natural and appealing when lit from above. Do not overlook the possibility of temporary outdoor lighting. If you have provided for an exterior socket, you can always add strings of lights.

Placing flares throughout a garden area, as in the garden above, provides a quick, inexpensive, portable way of introducing light.

A few examples of flares and candle-holders designed for outdoor use are illustrated on the right. The flickering quality of an open flame creates interesting shadows. Flares of many different heights can be bought.

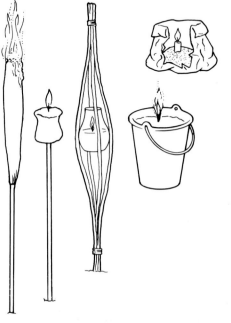

L·A·M·P·S & F·I·X·T·U·R·E·S

☐ A comprehensive guide to

available lighting tools

☐ Incandescent lamps

☐ Fluorescent lamps

☐ High Intensity Discharge lamps

☐ Specialized and decorative lamps

☐ Recessed and semi-recessed fixtures

☐ Wall washers, accent lights, track

☐ Surface-mounted fixtures, portable lights

☐ Pendants, wall lights, table lights

☐ Task lights, floor lights, exterior lights

☐ Controls, dimmers and switches

☐ Maintenance and storage

L·A·M·P·S

The heart of any lighting system is the source of light, the lamp. Thought of as 'bulbs' by the general public, they are called lamps by the lighting industry, which manufactures over 14,000 different types. That we should want to know and use only a few of these is like an artist wanting to use only two or three colors – possible, but not creative.

Lamps come in a bewildering array of shapes and sizes: they can be anything from 25mm to 2440mm long (1in–96in), with diameters from 6mm to 305mm ($\frac{1}{4}$in–12in). For precise information on a particular lamp, consult the maker's catalogue. Manufacturers are constantly developing new or improved lamps. Since lamps are the most important part of any lighting system, these developments are worth keeping up with.

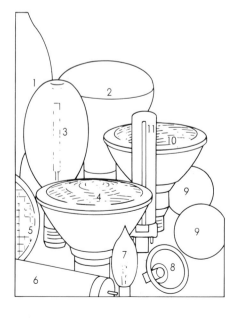

KEY   1 HID (metal halide) lamp
2 ER (Ellipsoidal Reflector) lamp
3 HID (sodium) lamp 4 HID (mercury PAR 38) lamp 5 PAR 36 lamp
6 Fluorescent lamps 7 Decorative lamp 8 Low-voltage dichroic reflector lamp 9 A lamps
10 PAR 38 lamp 11 PL lamp

HOW LIGHT IS MEASURED 1

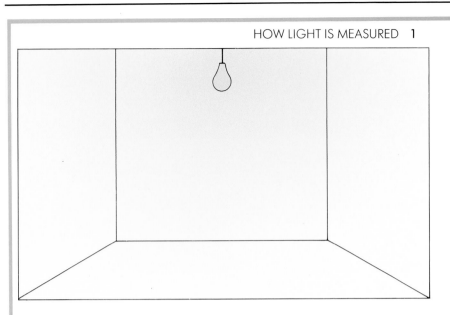

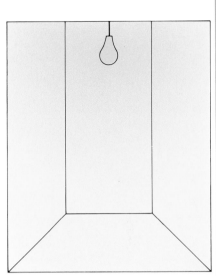

If you make use of manufacturers' catalogues – the principal source of information about lighting equipment – you will come across the same technical terms time and time again. You need to understand these terms to make an informed decision about your own lighting.

Watts Contrary to common misconception, watts have nothing at all to do with *light* energy. They measure the rate of *electrical* energy, as consumed by a hair drier, toaster, lamp, or whatever. While they are a guide to operating cost, the information they give about intensity applies only within families of lamps.

Lumens The lumen is the unit used to measure quantity, or intensity, of omni-directional light. An ordinary 75-watt A lamp (see page 78) produces 1190 lumens. A typical 20-watt fluorescent tube produces 1200 lumens. The two lamps produce almost the same amount of light, but the fluorescent tube uses a quarter of the energy of the incandescent lamp.

Lumens per watt (LPW) The relative energy-efficiency (or efficacy) of lamps is measured in LPW. Compare again the two lamps mentioned above: the A lamp produces 1190 lumens divided by 75 watts, which equals 15.87 lumens per watt (LPW); while the fluorescent tube produces $1200 \div 20 = 60$ LPW. You can see that the fluorescent tube is about four times more energy-efficient than the A lamp.

Footcandles (fc) are the measurement of illumination in lumens per square foot. Two spaces of different size may have the same number of lumens, but will have different fc levels (see example above).

Measuring fc levels The two spaces above – one of which is double the size of the other – are both lit by a lamp providing exactly the same number of lumens, 3000. While this seems a generous amount of light in the smaller space, the larger one feels dimly lit. This is because the number of fc, or lumens per square foot, is much lower in the larger space. In the space right, which is 6ft^2, or 36 square feet, there are 83.3 fc (3000 lumens ÷ 36 sq ft); in the space 12ft^2, or 144 square feet, there are only 20.9 fc (3000 ÷ 144).

The above formula is simplistic, because it takes no account of room height or reflectivity.

The chart on p. 132 gives both typical and recommended fc levels, and is intended to help you translate the figures into the light you see around you.

INCANDESCENT LAMPS
—TUNGSTEN—

In simple terms, the incandescent lamp works by the application of electrical energy to a thin wire filament, until it reaches incandescence – a temperature that causes the filament to glow.

Thomas Edison is credited with the first practical incandescent lamp, which was lit on 19 October 1879: the first light source to be commercially available.

From 1879 to the present day, incandescent light has been the source generally preferred. Examined objectively, this may seem surprising, as it is the least efficient source at converting electrical energy (watts) to light energy (lumens) (see page 77); its spectral distribution is weak at rendering colors in the blue family (see page 80); and, of all the light sources, it has the shortest life expectancy and the poorest lumen maintenance – at the end of its life an incandescent lamp delivers only 80 per cent of its initial lumen output.

So *why* is it universally preferred? There are several likely reasons. First, it has been available for longer than any other type. Second, its color distribution is heavily weighted towards the warm, orange-red end of the spectrum. People like the healthy look this gives them, reinforced by prejudice against early forms of fluorescent light (see page 89), which had poor color rendering at the warm end of the spectrum. Perhaps if fluorescent lamps had come first, they would be the norm by which color and appearance are judged.

A LAMPS

A 19

A 21

BASE	Edison Screw, Bayonet
WATTAGE	25–200
LUMENS	c.235–3150
FINISH	Clear, frosted, white, daylight, various colors.
TYPICAL APPLICATIONS	Used in majority of table and floor lamps, downlights, wall washers, and in fixtures with diffusers and shades.
COMMENTS	This is the 'standard' lamp by which we still judge all others. Its average life is from 750 to 1000 hours; its Kelvin temperature (see p.91) is typically 2600. Almost all lamp sizes have their diameter expressed in eights of an inch: thus an A 19 has a diameter of $\frac{19}{8}$in or $2\frac{3}{8}$in, and a PAR 38 is $4\frac{3}{4}$in. (For industrial application lamps are available up to 1000 watts.)
SCALE 1:4	

MUSHROOM LAMPS	SILVER BOWL LAMPS	T LAMPS (TUBULAR)	
		SINGLE BASE	DOUBLE BASE
Edison Screw, Bayonet	Edison Screw, Bayonet, Small Edison Screw	**a** S14d; **b** Edison Screw, Bayonet, Small Edison Screw, Candelabra Screw; **c** Bayonet; **d** S14s; **e** Disc; **f** S15s	
40–150	40–500	Single Base: 25–75; Double Base: 30–120	
c.235–2300	c.290–9500	c.165–840	
White	Silver or gold bowl, with clear or frosted bulb.	Clear, frosted.	
Used in same sorts of ways as an A lamp but offers more diffuse light.	Used in display fixtures and others that employ reflectors to redirect the light.	Used in display case lighting, around mirrors, and as concealed lighting in coves, soffits and under shelves	
The mushroom lamp's shape and diffuse light make it more suitable than ordinary A lamps for positions where the lamp is exposed. Life expectancy and Kelvin temperature are the same as for A lamps. Not a common lamp in the US.	Silver bowl lamps direct light up towards the reflector. The light is intensified and the beam reshaped by the reflector. With a diffuse reflector, the result is a soft, indirect light. Life expectancy and Kelvin temperature are the same as for A lamps.	These lamps are often known as architectural strip lamps. Except around mirrors, where their 'warm' light is valued, they are being replaced by more energy-efficient fluorescent tubes. **c** and **f** are not common in the US. Life expectancy and Kelvin temperature are the same as for A lamps.	

PARTS OF THE LAMP

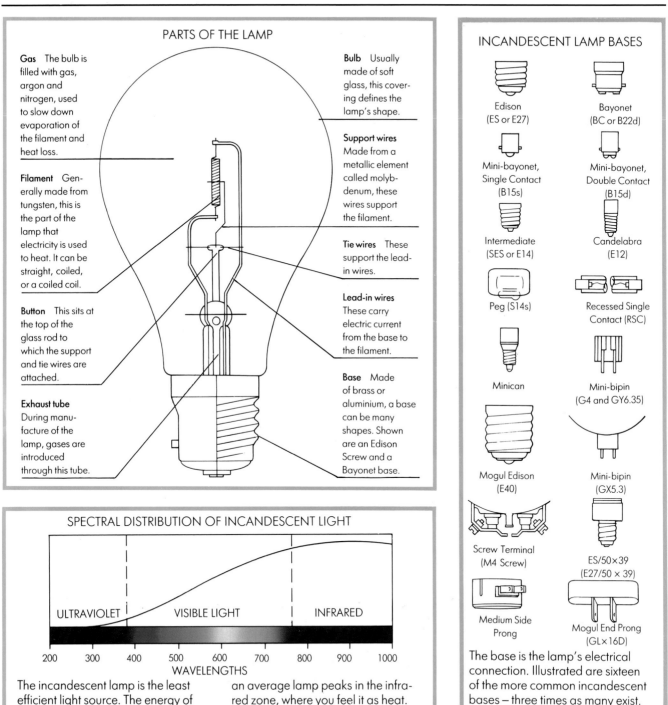

Gas The bulb is filled with gas, argon and nitrogen, used to slow down evaporation of the filament and heat loss.

Filament Generally made from tungsten, this is the part of the lamp that electricity is used to heat. It can be straight, coiled, or a coiled coil.

Button This sits at the top of the glass rod to which the support and tie wires are attached.

Exhaust tube During manufacture of the lamp, gases are introduced through this tube.

Bulb Usually made of soft glass, this covering defines the lamp's shape.

Support wires Made from a metallic element called molybdenum, these wires support the filament.

Tie wires These support the lead-in wires.

Lead-in wires These carry electric current from the base to the filament.

Base Made of brass or aluminium, a base can be many shapes. Shown are an Edison Screw and a Bayonet base.

INCANDESCENT LAMP BASES

Edison
(ES or E27)

Bayonet
(BC or B22d)

Mini-bayonet,
Single Contact
(B15s)

Mini-bayonet,
Double Contact
(B15d)

Intermediate
(SES or E14)

Candelabra
(E12)

Peg (S14s)

Recessed Single
Contact (RSC)

Minican

Mini-bipin
(G4 and GY6.35)

Mogul Edison
(E40)

Mini-bipin
(GX5.3)

Screw Terminal
(M4 Screw)

ES/50×39
(E27/50 × 39)

Medium Side
Prong

Mogul End Prong
(GL×16D)

The base is the lamp's electrical connection. Illustrated are sixteen of the more common incandescent bases – three times as many exist.

SPECTRAL DISTRIBUTION OF INCANDESCENT LIGHT

ULTRAVIOLET | VISIBLE LIGHT | INFRARED

WAVELENGTHS
200   300   400   500   600   700   800   900   1000

The incandescent lamp is the least efficient light source. The energy of an average lamp peaks in the infrared zone, where you feel it as heat.

HOW LIGHT IS MEASURED **2**

The following pages deal with 'display' lamps or 'spot' lights, designed to cast light in a specific direction. Spotlights are 'hotter' at the center of their beam: their light falls in a non-uniform distribution pattern. Lumens are not an appropriate measure for them.

Candelas The power or luminous intensity of directional lamps is measured in candelas, a term that expresses a lamp's candlepower. Whereas with omni-directional lamps you calculate footcandles by working out the number of lumens per square foot (see page 77), with directional lamps you work out the number of fc by dividing the square of distance between the source and lit object (also known as the inverse square law).

— 1 —

Beam and field angle The center of the beam is the area in which the lamp delivers 50% of its candlepower – the beam angle. Often this is the only measurement given in catalogues. But outside the beam angle is an area of 'spill' light, which has only 10% of the candlepower. The beam angle and spill light together add up to the field angle.

— 2 —

Candela distribution chart From this you can find out how much spill light your chosen lamp gives.

Shown is a typical 150-watt PAR 38 flood, with a maximum intensity of 2600 candelas. The beam angle is where 50% of maximum is still available – 1300 candelas. If you draw a line (A–B) through the point at which 1300 intersects the candela distribution line, you can see that the beam angle is 20° × 2 (to account for the symmetrical beam) = 40°.

The spill light is where 10% of full candlepower is still available – 260 candelas. If you draw a line (A–C) where 260 intersects the candela distribution line, you can see that the field angle is 30° × 2 = 60°.

— 3 —

Typical distribution cone Many manufacturers tell you the number of fc and the diameter covered by the beam angle at various distances from the source.

— 4 —

Applying your knowledge Assume you have a table 5ft in diameter that you want to light. It is 6ft from your light source. You look at a manufacturer's chart (**3**) to work out that a 150-watt PAR 38 flood will almost cover the area, providing a generous 72 fc.

If your table is close to a wall, with your light centered over the table, you may notice 'scallops' of light along your wall. You have not allowed for the spill light. The 40° beam angle exactly covers the table; the 60° field angle causes the light to hit the wall. If you do not want this to happen, either use a lamp or fixture with narrower distribution, or one with less spill light, or move light and table further away from the wall.

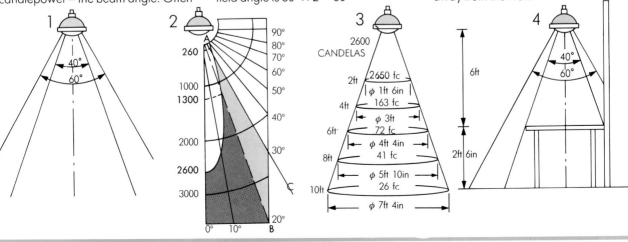

INCANDESCENT LAMPS
— DISPLAY —

Unlike ordinary incandescent lamps, display lamps are made to cast their beam of light in a specific direction. This characteristic gives them a number of advantages over A lamps and other omni-directional sources.

First, because they are made with an integral reflector they are a self-contained optical system. Second, because the lamp is a complete system, the fixtures don't need to contain a lens or reflector, so they can be smaller and cheaper. Finally, the lamp life is at least twice as long as A lamps (about 2000 hours). On the other hand, they are more expensive than lamps.

The term 'display lamp' refers in general to the three following categories:

1 R lamps Reflector lamps have a parabolic reflector (see page 128) coated with silver or with vaporized aluminium.

2 ER lamps The Ellipsoidal Reflector lamp was developed to function efficiently in deep recessed fixtures (see page 100). Its beam has two focal points, one at the filament and the other 50mm (2in) in front of the lamp. Because light is not trapped inside the fixture, less is wasted.

3 PAR lamps The term PAR is used to stand for Parabolic Aluminized Reflector.

Watt for watt PAR lamps give 50 per cent more directional light in spot and 300 per cent more light in flood than comparable R lamps. The latter, however, give you a wider, smoother, and softer light.

	R LAMPS (REFLECTOR)		
	R 20	R 30	R 40
NB Figures given are an average.			
BASE	Edison Screw, Bayonet	Edison Screw, Bayonet	
WATTAGE	30–60	75–100	75–300
BEAM ANGLE	35°	Flood: 78° Spot: 26°	Flood: 76° Spot: 22°
MAXIMUM CANDELAS	290–550	430–13,000	
TYPICAL APPLICATIONS	Used as an accent light at close quarters.	Used in all types of fixtures – directional task lights, downlights, wall washers, softer accent lights.	
COMMENTS	These are the most common R lamps, although certain manufacturers make smaller ones. The degree to which the front of the bulb is frosted determines whether the lamp will be a 'spot' or a 'flood'. Lamps are made from one piece of blown glass and are only suitable for indoor use. Being wider, softer, and dimmer than their PAR 38 counterparts, these lamps are more effective as general area lighting than true accent lighting. Sylvania offers a PAR 20 and a PAR 30.		
SCALE 1:4			

ER LAMPS (ELLIPSOIDAL REFLECTOR)	PAR LAMPS (PARABOLIC REFLECTOR)			
	PAR 38	PAR 46	PAR 56	PAR 64
Edison Screw	Edison Screw	Medium Side Prong	Mogul End Prong	Extended Mogul End Prong
50 & 75	75–150	200	300	500
28°	Flood: 30° Spot: 16°	Medium Flood: 11°–26° Narrow Spot: 9°–13°	Wide Flood: 19°–42° Medium Flood: 11°–23° Narrow Spot: 8°–10°	Wide Flood: 19°–58° Medium Flood: 9°–24° Narrow Spot: 7°–10°
1800–2900	Flood: 1500–2600 Spot: 3800–7500	Medium Flood: 11,200 Narrow Spot: 32,500	Wide Flood: 10,000 Medium Flood: 24,000 Narrow Spot: 70,000	Wide Flood: 12,000 Medium Flood: 35,000 Narrow Spot: 110,000
Used in deep recess fittings, where the front of the lamp is at least 45mm (1¾in) from the fixture's aperture.	Used in downlights, wall washers, accent lights, and outdoor fixtures.	Used in outdoor fixtures, or as accent lights in high ceilings.		
These were thought up as energy-saving replacements for the R lamp. As they are 20mm (¾in) longer than their R counterparts, they must not be used in shallow fittings, where they stick out and are a source of glare.	All PAR lamps are made of two pieces of glass fused together. One piece is the reflector, which is coated with a thin layer of vaporized aluminium, and the other part is the front lens. The way in which the lens is stippled determines the beam angle. Since both pieces are made of hard, heat-resistant glass, PAR lamps are suitable for use out of doors. The PAR 38 is the workhorse of the accent lights. Because of its popularity, many manufacturers offer lamps with improved reflector design, allowing the same lumens for fewer watts. The initial cost is higher. The beams from the PAR 46, 56, and 64 are oval in shape and can be re-oriented, since most lamps can be rotated with their fittings. Fixtures for these lamps are large and conspicuous. They are most often used out of doors and as strong accent lights over long distances, or to make bold statements.			

INCANDESCENT LAMPS
—LOW-VOLTAGE—

Because low-voltage lamps operate at less than line voltage, you will always need a 'step-down' transformer. In portable fixtures this is integral; often with recessed fixtures and track it is located separately. Most – not all – low-voltage lamps are made of tiny tungsten-halogen capsules cemented into a reflector.

How halogen lamps work In an ordinary incandescent lamp, the tungsten filament gradually evaporates and is deposited on the relatively cool bulb wall. This accounts for the darkened appearance of an old or burned-out lamp. The bulb of a tungsten-halogen lamp reaches a minimum temperature of 250°C (480°F), and can be as high as 1200°C (2190°F). The evaporated tungsten combines with the halogen to make a compound. As the compound approaches the bulb wall, the high heat drives it back to the filament, where the even higher temperature – around 3000°C or 5430°F – causes it to separate and the tungsten to be redeposited on the filament. This is known as the 'halogen regenerative cycle'. If the tungsten could be redeposited on the exact place it originally evaporated from, the lamp would last indefinitely.

	PAR 36	BARE LAMPS	
OPERATING VOLTAGE	5.5, 12	6, 12, 24	
BASE	M4 Screw	G4, GY6.35 (Mini-bipin)	
WATTAGE	25, 35, 50, 75, 100	5, 10, 20, 35, 50, 75, 100	
BEAM ANGLE	3°–60°	Not display lamps	
MAXIMUM CANDELAS	250–45,000	Measured in lumens: 60–2500	
COMMENTS	The tungsten PAR 36 was the original standard low-voltage accent light. With a life of 1500 to 2500 hours, its beam is distinctively oval. Some manufacturers offer halogen versions, with improved performance and increased cost.	These tiny lamps are used in many contemporary fixtures – from portable task lights to recessed, surface, and track accent lights. They are entirely dependent on a reflector to distribute their light. Some are available with axial filaments. Their miniature pin bases are fragile – handle them with care.	
SCALE 1:2.5			

Benefits of low voltage Those halogen and tungsten low-voltage lamps with an integral reflector share advantages with display lamps (see page 82). The shape and facets of the reflector determine the beam angle (see page 81).

Low-voltage halogen lamps have the same advantages as line voltage halogen lamps (see page 86). Additionally their compact filament allows a more precise alignment within the reflector, resulting in far less 'spill' light than line voltage lamps (see page 81). This improves their optical performance so that they can replace line voltage lamps twice their wattage. They also have a long lamp life of between 2000 and 4000 hours. Furthermore, their small size has led to a host of compact fixtures, which are easily recessed or concealed in shallow ceiling cavities (see page 100). However, there are a few disadvantages. You must take care that the wattage of your lamp does not exceed your transformer capacity; with a remotely located transformer, you would be wise to have your low-voltage system professionally installed to ensure an even power supply. The initial equipment cost is also higher than it is for line voltage lamps, partly because of the need for the transformer and partly because the lamps themselves are expensive.

REFLECTOR LAMPS

	MR 16	MR 11	
2in	1⅜in	56mm	70mm
12	12	6, 12, 24	12
GX5.3 (Mini-bipin)	G4, B15d (shown)	G4, B15d (shown)	B15d
20, 50, 75	20	10, 20	20, 50, 75
5°–40°	7° and 17°	6.5°–15°	10° and 30°
460–17,500	1760–4800	850–7500	600–15,000

MR stands for Multi-reflector (a common name). The number gives the diameter in eighths of an inch. In the past few years, over 30 of these lamps have been offered by various manufacturers – an expression of their confidence in, and rapid acceptance of, low-voltage technology. They can be bought wth dichroic reflectors, which make the light beam 60% cooler by directing the infrared spectrum (heat) out of the back of the lamp. Their wide range of beam spreads allows very precise accent light. The last two lamps illustrated are not very common in the US.

INCANDESCENT LAMPS
LINE VOLTAGE
—HALOGEN—

The tungsten-halogen lamp was introduced in the late 1950s. The bulb is filled with halogen gas; the lamp's high temperature initiates the 'halogen regenerative cycle' (see page 84).

Compared with standard tungsten lamps, halogen ones are far more efficient (as measured in LPW – see page 77). They give 95 per cent of their rated light output at the end of their life rather than the 80 per cent from A lamps, and their higher CCT (see page 91), as much as 3400K, gives them a far whiter appearance and an improved rendering of blue colors. Their life expectancy falls somewhere between 2000 and 4000 hours.

Because of their high temperature, fixtures must be designed to dissipate heat; you should also use caution when installing one near flammable wallcoverings. Avoid touching the bulb with bare hands, as small amounts of grease from your fingers reacting with the high bulb temperature can cause the quartz glass to lose its special properties, leading to early lamp failure.

	LINE VOLTAGE LINEAR LAMPS				PAR LAMPS·
	DOUBLE BASE		SINGLE BASE		PAR 38
BASE	RSC	RSC	Minican	Edison	Same as tungsten (p. 83)
WATTAGE	100–500	750–2000	100–500	150 and 250	90 and 250
LUMENS	1400–10,500	15,000–44,000	2500–11,500	2500 and 4200	Not applicable (see COMMENTS)
FINISH	Clear, frosted		Clear, frosted		Clear, or pebbled lens
TYPICAL APPLICATIONS	Used in fixtures with reflectors to give broad washes of light both indoors and outdoors.		Used in downlights, where higher fc levels than can be obtained from A lamps are wanted.		Used in same ways as tungsten PAR lamp (p. 83).
COMMENTS	As long as the reflector is well designed, the long filament gives an even light distribution, with minimum filament shadows or striations. Above 500 watts, these lamps should be positioned horizontally.		If these lamps are being used to replace A lamps, make sure the fixture can accommodate the higher temperatures of the halogen lamp.		PAR 56 (500 watts) and PAR 64 (1000 watts) are also available, in the same beam spreads as standard display lamps. Being directional lamps, their intensity is measured in candelas, not lumens.

SCALE
1:4

DISPLAY LAMPS DISTRIBUTION CHARTS

The charts on this page are for display lamps, as described on pages 82 and 85. Charts of this sort are often found in manufacturers' catalogues; they are used to give you a visual picture of the beam – the area covered by the light beam where you have 50 per cent of the lamp's maximum rated intensity – and of the lighting level in fc.

To make these charts useful, first work out the area of the object you want to light, then the distance from the lamp to that object. You will then be able to tell how precisely a particular lamp lights your chosen object, and what the fc level is.

If you are only given the candle-power rating, you can divide that by the square of the distance from source to object to find the number of fc at any point.

Remember that in the vast majority of catalogues the 'spill' light (10 per cent of the rated intensity – see page 81) is not given, but can be calculated.

F ∡ = Field angle
B ∡ = Beam angle
Cnt Cd = Maximum central candelas

1. Cnt Cd = 7500
F ∡ = 30°
B ∡ = 15°

2. Cnt Cd = 3100
F ∡ = 60°
B ∡ = 30°

3. Cnt Cd = 5400
F ∡ = 49°
B ∡ = 22°

4. Cnt Cd = 1040
F ∡ = 124°
B ∡ = 76°

5. Cnt Cd = 3300
F ∡ = 13°
B ∡ = 10°

6. Cnt Cd = 460
F ∡ = 37°
B ∡ = 36°

7. Cnt Cd = 9150
F ∡ = 13°
B ∡ = 11°

8. Cnt Cd = 2700
F ∡ = 27°
B ∡ = 22°

1 150W PAR 38 SPOT

Fc	Distance
1875	2ft
469	4ft
208	6ft
117	8ft
75	10ft

4ft 2ft 0 2ft 4ft

2 150W PAR 38 FLOOD

Fc	Distance
775	2ft
194	4ft
86	6ft
48	8ft
31	10ft

6ft 4ft 2ft 0 2ft 4ft 6ft

3 150W R 40 SPOT

Fc	Distance
1350	2ft
338	4ft
150	6ft
84	8ft
54	10ft

6ft 4ft 2ft 0 2ft 4ft 6ft

4 150W R 40 FLOOD

Fc	Distance
260	2ft
65	4ft
29	6ft
16	8ft
10	10ft

8ft 6ft 4ft 2ft 0 2ft 4ft 6ft 8ft

5 20W/12 VOLT REFLECTOR SPOT

Fc	Distance
825	2ft
206	4ft
92	6ft
52	8ft
33	10ft

2ft 0 2ft

6 20W/12VOLT REFLECTOR FLOOD

Fc	Distance
115	2ft
29	4ft
13	6ft
7	8ft
5	10ft

4ft 2ft 0 2ft 4ft

7 50W/12VOLT REFLECTOR SPOT

Fc	Distance
2288	2ft
872	4ft
254	6ft
143	8ft
92	10ft

2ft 0 2ft

8 50W/12VOLT REFLECTOR FLOOD

Fc	Distance
675	2ft
169	4ft
75	6ft
42	8ft
27	10ft

4ft 2ft 0 2ft 4ft

DECORATIVE LAMPS

Decorative lamps are usually exposed. They are intended to be luminous decorative elements rather than the main source of light in a room. Small lamps will make your chandelier sparkle as each facet picks up the filament image. Your room will gain in interest and atmosphere, but the general light will be dim and diffuse – decorative lamps will hardly ever provide enough light to lend interest to a room's architecture or occupants. With the exception of globe lamps, which can be anything from 25 to 150 watts, they rate low wattage (15 to 60 watts), low efficiency, and low lumens.

There are thousands of different decorative lamps. Some are designed to simulate candle flames, using a flickering filament. Others are meant to look like old-fashioned gas or oil lamps. They can be as small as your fingernail (see page 96) or large as a 127mm (5in) globe lamp.

Quite apart from the major manufacturers, many smaller firms fabricate specialized 'decor' lamps. The worldwide variations are endless, and any lamps sharing the same voltage and base can be interchanged. They are also long lived, lasting for 1500 to 4000 hours. Just as well, because decorative lamps are often expensive.

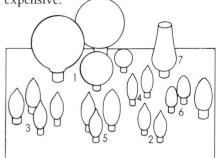

KEY 1 Globe lamps 2 Straight-tipped lamps 3 Bent-tipped lamps 4 Flicker lamps 5 'Gas' lamps 6 'Flame' lamps 7 'Chimney' lamp

FLUORESCENT LAMPS

The first fluorescent lamp to be commercially available was introduced to the public at the New York World Fair in 1939. The scientific community was excited to find that fluorescent light was four times more efficient than incandescent light (see page 77), with a lamp life 10 to 20 times as long.

But the general public was less than happy with fluorescent light. The major complaint had to do with the unfamiliar color rendering. In the early days this was a fair criticism, but the manufacturers have worked very hard in recent years to produce fluorescent lamps with a color rendering corresponding as closely as possible to the 'familiar' standard of the warm incandescent lamp.

The other main complaint concerns the quality of the light. By design, fluorescent lamps are sources

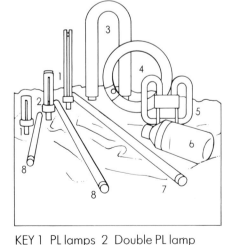

KEY 1 PL lamps 2 Double PL lamp
3 U-shaped lamp 4 Circular lamp
5 2-D lamp 6 SL lamp 7 Linear tube
8 Miniature tubes

of diffused light. Although ideal where you want an even wash of concealed light that is small in size and low in heat – such as above counter tops or in coves – they can never be sources of accent lighting. The more recent compact fluorescents (see page 92), while competitive in size with incandescent (filament) lamps, are still not accent light.

Several other prejudices are now also out of date. In the early days the ballast or conntrol gear that all fluorescent lamps need was very noisy and tended to leak black resin. This is now only a problem in the very cheapest of fixtures. Electronic and lead-lag ballast have also eliminated the flickering effect and buzz that many people found irritating. Studies indicate that the ultraviolet radiation in fluorescent light is not harmful. Most complaints are the result of poor design application.

HOW VISIBLE LIGHT IS PRODUCED

Fluorescent light depends on establishing an electric arc in a gaseous environment. Turning on the electricity heats the cathodes, which release streams of electrons. These create an electric current and collide with mercury atoms vaporized by the heat. The 'excited' atoms return to their normal state immediately and, in the process, release energy in a specific spectrum of ultraviolet light, which the eye does not see. However, the phosphor coating reacts to the ultraviolet radiation and is caused to fluoresce, producing visible light. The color of the light produced is dependent on the make-up of the phosphor coating.

LINEAR FLUORESCENTS

Linear fluorescents are most commonly used in the home to light counters and other large work surfaces, or as hidden lighting to highlight architectural features. The tube, the first type of fluorescent lamp to be developed, is still the most common. Its length gives off a large volume of diffused light. Since the light is distributed in all directions, you need a housing, reflector, or lens/louvre to control it (see page 128).

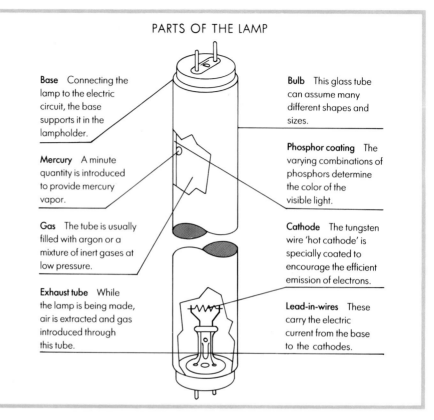

PARTS OF THE LAMP

Base Connecting the lamp to the electric circuit, the base supports it in the lampholder.

Mercury A minute quantity is introduced to provide mercury vapor.

Gas The tube is usually filled with argon or a mixture of inert gases at low pressure.

Exhaust tube While the lamp is being made, air is extracted and gas introduced through this tube.

Bulb This glass tube can assume many different shapes and sizes.

Phosphor coating The varying combinations of phosphors determine the color of the visible light.

Cathode The tungsten wire 'hot cathode' is specially coated to encourage the efficient emission of electrons.

Lead-in-wires These carry the electric current from the base to the cathodes.

Tubes are available in two diameters, 26mm (1in) and 38mm ($1\frac{1}{2}$in), and in a wide range of lengths – 600mm (2ft) to 2400mm (8ft). You can also buy miniature tubes 16mm ($\frac{5}{8}$in) in diameter, anywhere from 150mm (6in) to 525mm (1ft 9in) long. The intensity of linear tubes is related to their length. It is now possible to dim most fluorescent lamps.

These lamps need long fixtures to accommodate them; recessed invariably they run into some obstacle.

LAMP COMPATIBILITY

Where a linear fixture comes complete with a lamp, the lamp supplied will probably be the cheapest – 'cool white'. As this is the one under which warm colors and people's complexions suffer, you may want to change the lamp. Lamps with improved color rendering are available.

To make sure a new lamp is compatible with its fixture, bear the following points in mind:
1 The lamp's wattage, which is determined by tube length and diameter, and which needs to be compatible with the ballast capacity;
2 The type of ballast, which can be 'switchstart', 'rapid start', or, rarely, 'instant start';
3 The Power Factor of the lamp, which can be High (HPF), Low (LPF), or Very High (VHPF);

Correlated Color Temperature (CCT) A way of measuring the difference between fluorescent light colors is by referring to temperature. If you heat a piece of metal, it glows in sequence – red, yellow, blue, blue-white. Its temperature at any color can be measured in degrees Kelvin (K). The lower the number, the 'warmer' the look of the light source; the higher the number, the 'cooler' its appearance. (The term 'correlated' is used because metal temperature cannot be measured above 5000K, so an agreed color of daylight is used.)

CHART OF CCT

Incandescent lamp	2600K–3200K
Warm White (WW) and Deluxe Warm White (WWX) fluorescent lamps	3000K
Cool White (CW) and Deluxe Cool White (CWX) fluorescent lamps	4200K
Daylight fluorescent lamp	7000K
Sunlight at sunrise	1800K
Sunlight at noon	5000K
Overcast sky	6500K
Blue (clear northwest) sky	25,000K

The CCT of a lamp is a rough guide to the color of the light source itself, as it appears to you. The fluorescent WW and WWX both have CCTs of 3000K – in the same range as standard incandescents – but colors do not appear the same under these three sources.

HOW COLOR IS MEASURED

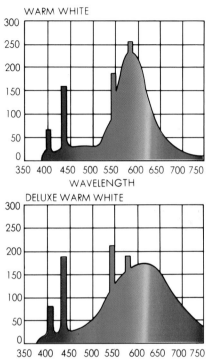

Different types of lamps are made up of different wavelengths in the color spectrum. In manufacturers' catalogues, the color output of a lamp is known as its spectral distribution. Illustrated here are the spectral distributions of two lamps with the same CCT – Warm White and Deluxe Warm White. You can see what a difference there is in the colors being emitted. The WW has very little orange-red and lots of green-yellow, while the WWX has much improved red-orange and not as much yellow-green. (Neither has as much orange-red as incandescent, which also has less yellow-green – see p. 80).

Color Rendering Index A third system of color measurement is known as the Color Rendering Index. Eight pastel colors are put under a light source and the degree to which these colors shift by comparison with two defined references determines the index of the light source. The two references are (a) Incandescent light, given a rating of 100 (yet incandescent light lacks blue color output); (b) North sky light at 7500K, also given a rating of 100 (north sky light is deficient in red).

The CRI is only a valuable guide when you are examining lamps with a comparable color temperature. If you look again at the chart, you will see that it is fair to compare WW, WWX, and incandescent lamps, because their CCTs are all within 300K of each other. They rate 52, 77, and 100 respectively on the CRI. On the other hand, it is not fair to compare the good CRI – 89 – of CWX with the others, because its CCT is more than 1000K different.

COLOR RENDERING OF DIFFERENT LINEAR FLUORESCENTS (VERSUS INCANDESCENT)						
LAMP	LUMENS PER WATT (LPW)	COLOR RENDERING INDEX (CRI)	CORRELATED COLOR TEMPERATURE (CCT)	WHITENESS	COLORS ENHANCED	COLORS GREYED
INCAN (100 W)	17.5	99+	2900	Yellowish	Deep Red, Red, Orange, Yellow	Blue, Green
WARM WHITE (WW)	80.0	52	3000	Yellowish	Orange, Yellow	Red, Blue, Green
COOL WHITE (CW)	78.8	62	4150	White White	Yellow, Orange, Blue	Red
DELUXE COOL WHITE (CWX)	56.3	89	4175	White (Pinkish)	All	None
DELUXE WARM WHITE (WWX)	55.0	77	3025	Yellowish	Red, Orange, Yellow, Green	Blue
PLANT LIGHT	21.3	−2	6750	Purplish	Blue, Deep Red	Green, Yellow

4 The special ballast often needed if you want to dim the lamp;
5 The lamp base, which needs to be compatible with the socket of the fixture, but of which there are few.

This may seem a lot to consider, but major manufacturers make lamps throughout their range that meet the above combination of factors.

COMPACT FLUORESCENTS

Given the improved color and energy-efficiency, lamp manufacturers knew they were on to a good thing with fluorescent light. They began to work on ways of tapping the domestic and commercial markets. The compact fluorescent was the result.

The linear tube was bent, first into a circular, then into a U-shape; more recently, further bends and twists have been added, producing the many different shapes known as PL, SL, and 2-D.

Circular lamps The first non-linear shapes to be developed, these had dull and badly conceived fixtures. They became the poor relation of incandescents, their cheap efficiency causing them to end up in kitchens, bathrooms, and hallways of apartment complexes. Even now, few attractive fixtures have been designed

This chart takes five fluorescent lamps, which are common to most manufacturers, and compares their color characteristics and efficiency with the characteristics of incandescent light. (The newer lamps with improved color rendering are not shown on this list because they all have different trade names: look at manufacturers' catalogues for details.)

for them, so their potential has never been realized.

PL lamps Now both widely used and accepted, major companies have designed downlights for PL lamps, suitable for halls and other areas where high light levels are not needed. Many contemporary task and reading lamps have also been designed around this lamp.

SL lamps Unlike most PL lamps, which require control gear in the fixture, the SL lamp has a tiny electronic ballast built into it, making it totally self-contained. Its ease of use and the quality of its light make it a good A lamp replacement in standard table and floor lamps where dimming is not usually required, as well as in awkward places.

PL and SL lamps are both rated to work at low temperature, so they are suited to outdoor security lighting. Their much higher initial cost is offset by the fact that they last between 5 and 10 times as long as A lamps, and run on a lower wattage for the same amount of light.

2-D lamps This design is unique to Thorn EMI. In order to promote interest in their product, Thorn sponsored a design competition and succeeded in inspiring some exciting fixtures for the lamp.

All these compact lamps are highly suitable for the domestic market, but not enough attractive fixtures have yet been designed to make them prime choices. And, however compact, like all fluorescent lamps they remain diffuse sources, and can never be optically controlled point sources like the incandescents with which they are competing.

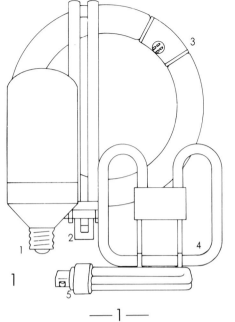

—1—

KEY 1 SL lamp 2 PL lamp
3 Circular lamp 4 2-D lamp
5 Double PL lamp

—2—

An exploded view of the SL lamp shows its component parts. Rated at 18 watts, it gives off 1100 lumens. This makes it competitive with a 75-watt A lamp, although its length of 183mm ($7\frac{1}{4}$in) makes it 70mm ($2\frac{3}{4}$in) longer. You can also buy 9-, 13-, and 25-watt versions; these compare favorably with 40-, 60-, and 100-watt A lamps.

—3—

Adaptors allow you to use an ordinary A lampholder with different fluorescent lamps. **a** is for a PL lamp, **b** for a circular lamp, and **c** for a 2-D lamp. All have built-in ballasts. Before you buy, consider the size of the old lamp, the size of the new, and the size of the adaptor; that way you will not end up with a lamp sticking out beyond the end of the shade.

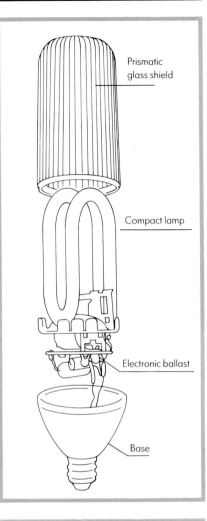

Prismatic glass shield

Compact lamp

Electronic ballast

Base

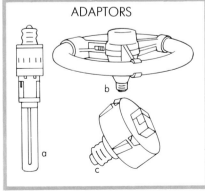

ADAPTORS

HIGH INTENSITY DISCHARGE LAMPS

HID lamps have been in use since the early 1930s, but the most exciting advances have occurred in the last ten years. They are very efficient lamps and deserve consideration in this energy-conscious age.

Simplistically, HID lamps produce light by means of a high-pressure arc discharge between electrodes, in an atmosphere of various gas vapors. Like an incandescent filament, some HID arcs are compact enough to be controlled optically with reflectors, housings, lenses, and so on.

There are disadvantages. The most important one from a domestic viewpoint is the unfamiliar color rendering of most HID lamps. But this will undoubtedly improve in the next few years. Another problem is the 'warm up' time needed before HID lamps reach full intensity and the 'cool down' time they need after being turned off. And, like fluorescents,

1

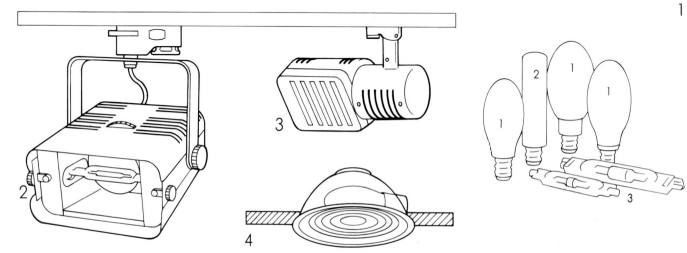

94

they need ballast or starter gear, although there are some self-ballasted mercury lamps.

There are three types of HID lamp. **Metal halide lamps** Prime candidates for residential use, the efficiency of these lamps is rated at about 60 to 100 LPW. A 70- or 150-watt metal halide lamp can replace a 150- or 300-watt incandescent. Their life expectancy is from 7500 to 15,000 hours, but their chief advantage is improved color rendering. The addition of halides to the gas vapor inside the bulb has made phosphor coatings unnecessary, so the light is less diffuse and more precise optical control is possible. Warm lamps with a CCT of 3000K have a CRI of 82, which is a satisfactory combination (see page 91). These are becoming very common in shop windows.

Mercury lamps About half as energy-efficient as metal halide, rating about 30 to 60 LPW, these lamps have an extraordinary long life of more than 24,000 hours, almost twice that of fluorescents. *Clear* mercury lamps have poor color rendering but, as with fluorescents, coating the bulbs with phosphor allows more pleasing visible colors. In general the only practical domestic application is as outdoor or security lighting.

High-pressure sodium lamps These are the most efficient lamps around, up to 140 lumens per watt. They have long life (12,000 to 24,000 hours) and excellent lumen maintenance. At present their residential use is limited to security lighting. However, much improved color rendering is soon promised.

5

NEON LAMPS

Neon, as decorative luminal art in the home, is making a comeback. Available from manufacturers only, neon's beautiful colors are the result of the gas used inside the tube and/or the phosphor coatings. You can bend the tubes into every imaginable design, but take care, as a large mass can be glaringly bright. Neon requires control gear. It can be dimmed.

COLD CATHODE LAMPS

Similar in quality and appearance to fluorescent light, cold cathode is a far more practical light source than neon. Like neon, it can easily be formed into long lengths of any shape, making it well suited to lighting intricate architectural forms, but it gives off more light. Easily dimmed, it has a very long life, although replacing lamp section is expensive. Control gear or ballasts are needed.

1

1 Mercury lamps 2 High-pressure sodium lamp 3 Metal halide lamps.

2

This fixture uses low-wattage metal halide lamps and has integral starter gear. The beam can be controlled from 'spot to flood'.

3

The mercury vapor lamp in this wall washer has integral control gear and a louvre for glare control.

4

This recessed lensed downlight looks exactly like an incandescent fixture, but is designed to take a mercury vapor lamp with external control gear.

5

The extensive use of neon, appropriately dimmed to avoid glare, is the focal point of this living room.

SPECIALIZED LAMPS

A fair proportion of all lamps fall into a 'special interest' category, and many of these can only be found in specialized catalogues. Such lamps usually have highly specific beam shapes and/or light characteristics; they are often low-voltage, with relatively short lives.

Designing lamps as the answer to specific problems can lead to unique solutions, which may then be more generally applied. For example, you might find a 12-volt tractor lamp with a very precise rectangular beam designed to illuminate rows of corn; you might then be able to use it successfully as a picture light.

ROUGH SERVICE AND VIBRATION LAMPS

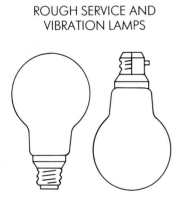

Rough service lamps have extra filament supports, making them suitable for portable work fixtures where they are liable to be jostled about. Vibration lamps – as their name suggests – have a specially wound filament allowing them to function near a source of vibration. Both types of lamp have low efficiency and a rated life of 1000 hours.

APPLIANCE LAMPS

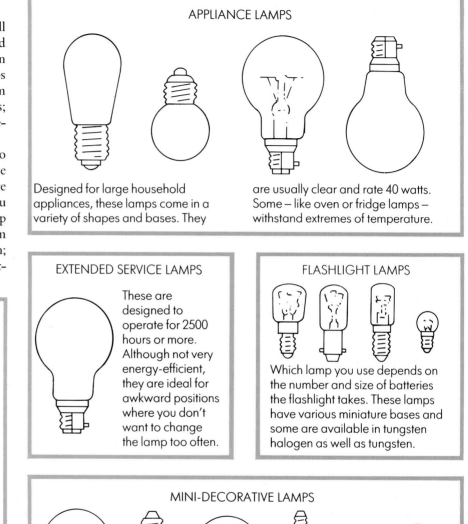

Designed for large household appliances, these lamps come in a variety of shapes and bases. They are usually clear and rate 40 watts. Some – like oven or fridge lamps – withstand extremes of temperature.

EXTENDED SERVICE LAMPS

These are designed to operate for 2500 hours or more. Although not very energy-efficient, they are ideal for awkward positions where you don't want to change the lamp too often.

FLASHLIGHT LAMPS

Which lamp you use depends on the number and size of batteries the flashlight takes. These lamps have various miniature bases and some are available in tungsten halogen as well as tungsten.

MINI-DECORATIVE LAMPS

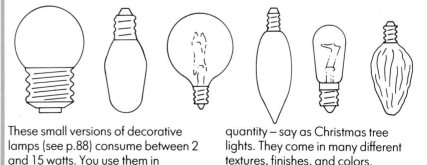

These small versions of decorative lamps (see p.88) consume between 2 and 15 watts. You use them in quantity – say as Christmas tree lights. They come in many different textures, finishes, and colors.

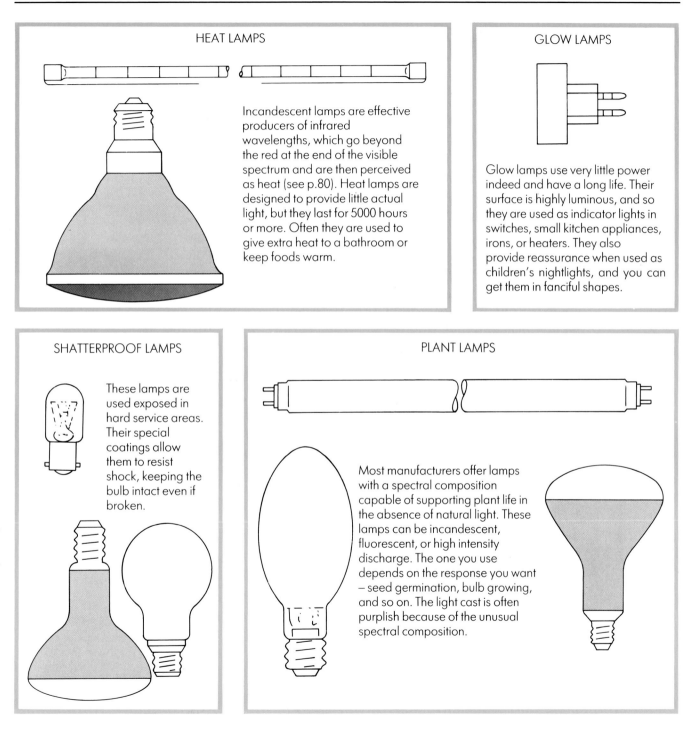

HEAT LAMPS

Incandescent lamps are effective producers of infrared wavelengths, which go beyond the red at the end of the visible spectrum and are then perceived as heat (see p.80). Heat lamps are designed to provide little actual light, but they last for 5000 hours or more. Often they are used to give extra heat to a bathroom or keep foods warm.

GLOW LAMPS

Glow lamps use very little power indeed and have a long life. Their surface is highly luminous, and so they are used as indicator lights in switches, small kitchen appliances, irons, or heaters. They also provide reassurance when used as children's nightlights, and you can get them in fanciful shapes.

SHATTERPROOF LAMPS

These lamps are used exposed in hard service areas. Their special coatings allow them to resist shock, keeping the bulb intact even if broken.

PLANT LAMPS

Most manufacturers offer lamps with a spectral composition capable of supporting plant life in the absence of natural light. These lamps can be incandescent, fluorescent, or high intensity discharge. The one you use depends on the response you want – seed germination, bulb growing, and so on. The light cast is often purplish because of the unusual spectral composition.

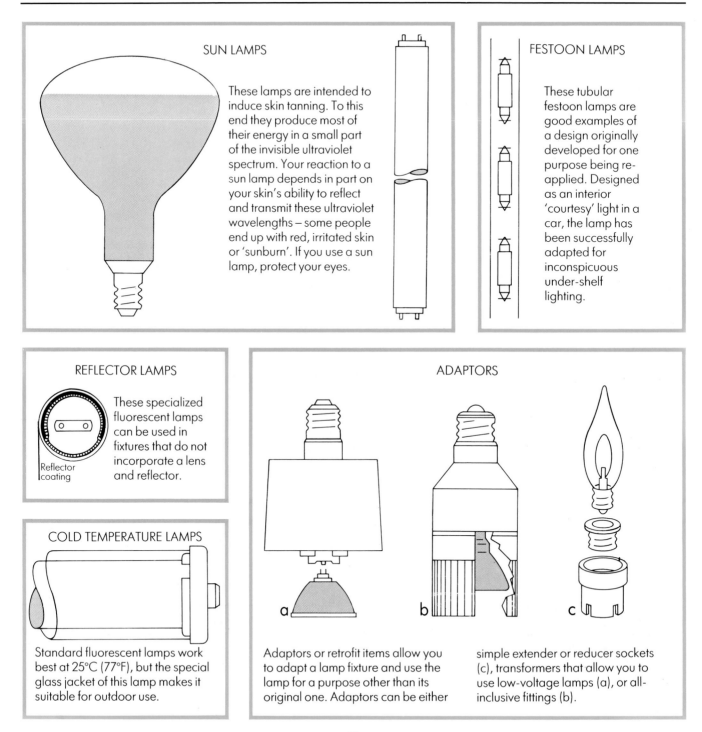

SUN LAMPS

These lamps are intended to induce skin tanning. To this end they produce most of their energy in a small part of the invisible ultraviolet spectrum. Your reaction to a sun lamp depends in part on your skin's ability to reflect and transmit these ultraviolet wavelengths – some people end up with red, irritated skin or 'sunburn'. If you use a sun lamp, protect your eyes.

FESTOON LAMPS

These tubular festoon lamps are good examples of a design originally developed for one purpose being re-applied. Designed as an interior 'courtesy' light in a car, the lamp has been successfully adapted for inconspicuous under-shelf lighting.

REFLECTOR LAMPS

These specialized fluorescent lamps can be used in fixtures that do not incorporate a lens and reflector.

Reflector coating

COLD TEMPERATURE LAMPS

Standard fluorescent lamps work best at 25°C (77°F), but the special glass jacket of this lamp makes it suitable for outdoor use.

ADAPTORS

a b c

Adaptors or retrofit items allow you to adapt a lamp fixture and use the lamp for a purpose other than its original one. Adaptors can be either simple extender or reducer sockets (c), transformers that allow you to use low-voltage lamps (a), or all-inclusive fittings (b).

—BEAMS OF LIGHT—

These photographs were taken to demonstrate the different qualities of the principal incandescent light sources. Smoke was used to make the light show up clearly. You can see that the smoke appears much brighter nearer the lamp. This is because of the inverse square law of light (see page 81). Since the camera is nowhere near as sensitive as the eye, the spill light (also defined on page 81) is not as clearly visible in the photographs as it would be in reality.

—1—

The R lamp counts as a display lamp. But you will notice that its light beam is very wide and the quality of light is much softer than that of the PAR or low-voltage lamps. It is not a good choice for true accent lighting. It also has the most spill light.

—2—

This 150-watt A lamp is housed in a reflector, which determines its beam spread. The quality of light is soft and the intensity is essentially even from edge to edge. The A lamp is well suited to areas of general illumination.

—3—

You can see that the center beam of the PAR 38 shown here is more intense than the R lamp's and there is also less spill light. As a result it is a truer accent light.

—4—

A 50-watt 12-volt lamp in a narrow angle reflector (6°) gives the most intense beam of the four. The more precise alignment of the tiny filament in relation to the reflector makes for the least amount of spill light. This lamp is ideally suited to accurate pinpointing of objects or art.

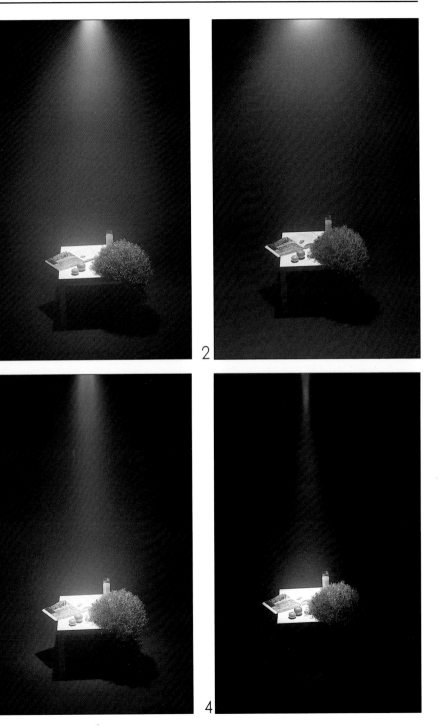

R·E·C·E·S·S·E·D F·I·X·T·U·R·E·S

The apparatus that holds the lamp and connects it to the source of power is officially known internationally as a 'luminaire'. More generally it is described as a fixture, a fitting, a lamp, or a lighting unit.

CHOOSING RECESSED — FIXTURES —

The use of recessed fixtures means that you have to know exactly what it is you want to light, because once the fixtures are installed you cannot easily move them.

The cost of a recessed fixture is normally related to the quality of the materials used to make it. Better materials last longer, and high-quality fixtures are easier to install. Units designed for A lamps, fluorescent, and bare halogen lamps depend on their reflectors to distribute the light, so the quality of the reflector is very important (see page 128).

The other main feature of any fixture is to minimize glare by shielding the light source (lamp) from view. When you are looking straight in front of you, your forehead acts as a visor: there is a 45° cut-off point beyond which direct glare does not affect you (unless you look up). To avoid direct glare, most fixtures are designed to shield the lamp within that 45° zone. A lot of cheap fixtures, however, fail to do this – for instance, often the lamp is placed too close to the aperture (the hole in the ceiling), the reflectors are poorly designed, or the baffles are inefficient at keeping light out of your eyes.

Recessed or flush-mounted fixtures Given the choice, most lighting designers prefer to use recessed or flush-mounted fixtures, because they best serve the magic quality of light. The light source is hidden, while the reflector and baffle minimize the apparent brightness at the opening. Only that which you choose to illuminate is revealed.

Recessed fixtures are usually fixed, but adjustable accent units are available. The latter allow you to direct light at angles up to 45°, although this does not mean that they are a panacea for indecision. Because of the problem of glare, their placement needs to be as well thought out as if they were fixed-recess fixtures.

Semi-recessed fixtures These are really a compromise choice when shallow ceiling cavities make it impossible to recess a fixture fully. You have to be careful about glare: it is a common failing of semi-recessed fixtures to have the lamp too close to the aperture. The great majority of available semi-recessed fixtures are also adjustable, which makes up for the fact that you have less choice than with fully recessed fixtures.

How you choose As the next few pages show, recessed and semi-recessed fittings, both fixed and adjustable, are made to accommodate all types of lamps; they provide beam spreads and light levels to suit every conceivable situation. It is impossible for lighting stores to carry the complete lines of all the available brands, so consult some of the manufacturers' catalogues. These will provide you with the information you need to decide what fixture and lamp combination is best suited to your particular need. Catalogues give all physical measurements – a key factor in determining what you can use.

If you want to renovate the lighting in your present home, you need to find out the depth of your ceiling cavity. This is critical in determining which recessed units you can use, or whether you can use them at all. If you are having a house built for you, see if you can reverse the normal procedure: try and make sure that your ceiling cavities will accommodate your chosen light fixtures.

If you have 210mm ($8\frac{1}{4}$in) of space above your ceiling, you will find that there is a wide selection of fixtures to choose from. With 305mm (12in) of space, you can choose almost any recessed fixture. At the other end of the scale, a minimal clearance of 135mm ($5\frac{3}{8}$in) allows you to use side-mounted lamps and a few low-voltage units that have remotely or separately located transformers.

Bear in mind that there is nothing to prevent the creative use of recessed fixtures in walls or floors, as long as their brightness and glare are both adequately controlled.

AN A LAMP

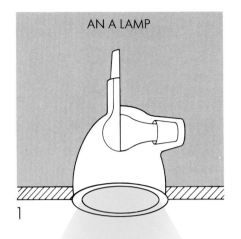

1

55°

LOW-VOLTAGE LAMP

2

10°

R LAMP

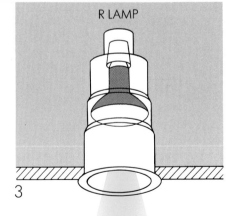

3

28°

PAR 38 LAMP

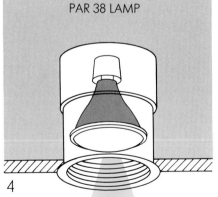

4

36°

—1—

These downlights depend on their reflectors to redirect the light. As well as using vertically mounted lamps, you can use horizontally mounted ones (so they fit in shallow ceiling cavities). Always use the specified lamp, because the efficiency of the reflector depends on a precise filament position.

—2—

The low-voltage lamp shown here has an integral transformer. If you choose a lamp with a remotely located transformer, it will take up less depth (130mm or $5\frac{1}{4}$in); this means you can install recessed fixtures in very shallow ceiling cavities. The lamp is also the optical system.

—3—

The lamp is the optical system (contains its own reflector), so the depth of the cone or baffle determines the amount of spill light trapped inside the fixture. Units where the lamp is too near the opening can be glaring.

—4—

Similar in concept to the R lamp downlight **3**, this one has an annular ring baffle to limit spill light. The more effective units have a lamp that is deeply recessed.

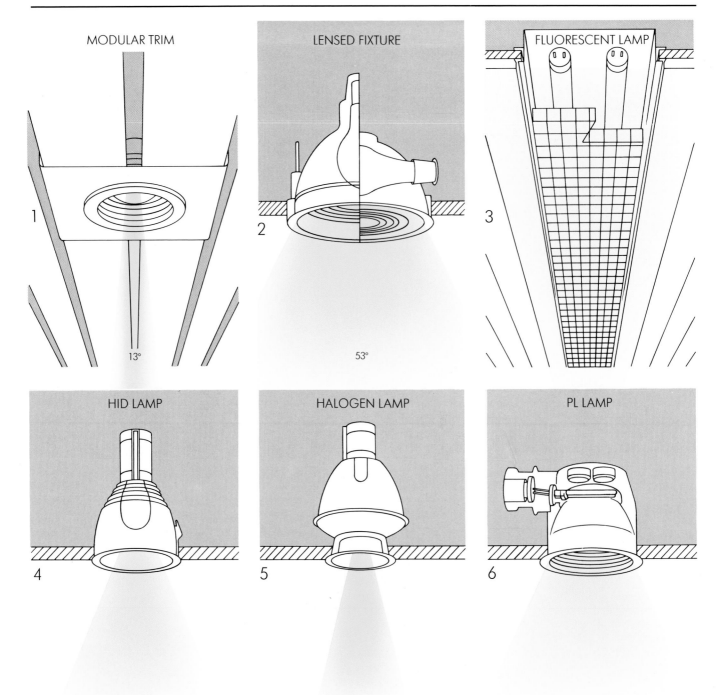

MODULAR TRIM

1

13°

LENSED FIXTURE

2

53°

FLUORESCENT LAMP

3

HID LAMP

4

46°

HALOGEN LAMP

5

28°

PL LAMP

6

50°

— 1 —

These fixtures are designed so that the 'trims' align with specific modular ceiling designs. Shown here is a fixture for narrow aluminium slats.

— 2 —

The addition of a lens or diffuser to a fixture for an A lamp produces a soft, wide beam. Lensed fixtures are most useful in low ceilings or for lighting large areas with low light levels.

— 3 —

Recessed fixtures for fluorescent lamps are quite shallow on average – 125mm (5in). Their sizes are related to the length of tube used, but a single tube only needs an opening of 125mm (5in). The unit illustrated has a louvre with a 45° cut-off point.

— 4 —

Units for HID lamps have remote control gear (not shown) and are available in similar design to standard A lamp fittings. Gold-colored reflectors help warm up the cool light of HID lamps, which can be vertically or horizontally mounted.

— 5 —

Because of the high heat produced by halogen lamps, most fixtures for them are too large and deep for ordinary domestic ceilings. Their higher light output makes halogen suitable for spaces with high ceilings.

— 6 —

A new generation of recessed downlights incorporates the PL lamp, with integral control gear. Silver or gold reflectors (for warmer light) are normally offered. Giving diffuse light over a large area, these lamps are useful for low ceilings and areas of low light levels.

ADJUSTABLE FIXTURES

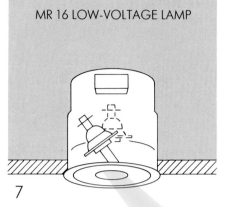

MR 16 LOW-VOLTAGE LAMP

7

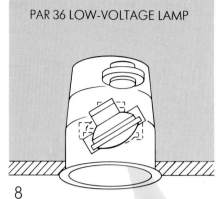

PAR 36 LOW-VOLTAGE LAMP

8

10°   20°

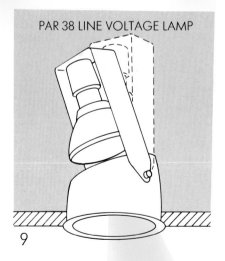

PAR 38 LINE VOLTAGE LAMP

9

30°

— 7 —

These small lamps now allow accent lights to be recessed in shallow cavities. If the transformer is located separately, the cavity depth can be as shallow as 135mm ($5\frac{3}{8}$in). MR 16 lamps offer a wider choice of beam spreads and less spill light than a PAR 38. You can direct them to 45°.

— 8 —

Fixtures for PAR 36 low-voltage lamps have similar advantages to MR 16s, except that you can only focus a PAR 36 to 35°. (These fittings can accommodate 5.5 volt 'pin' spots with a 5° beam angle.)

— 9 —

This fixture takes a line voltage PAR 38, with its wide range of wattages. You need a cavity depth of at least 203mm (8in).

— 1 —

This fixture can be fully recessed or fully exposed depending on your ceiling depth. The illustrated trim is square; round ones are also available.

— 2 —

The classic swivelling 'eyeball' shown here is designed to accommodate mercury vapor HID lamps with remotely located control gear.

— 3 —

This fixture can swivel 30° in all directions. The housing is adjustable, making it ideal for sloped ceilings.

— 4 —

A clever low-voltage accent light, this fixture can swing up flush with the ceiling and act as a downlight or be adjusted through 90°.

— 5 —

Using a silver bowl lamp and a parabolic reflector, this accent light creates an intense narrow beam of light. It is adjustable in all directions and can be flush with the ceiling. The transformer can be part of the unit or remotely located.

— 6 —

This is the line voltage counterpart to **5**. Two reflector designs are available, one for narrow beam and one for wide.

— 7 —

This fixture uses a linear halogen lamp and gives a wide dispersion of light. It is well suited for wall washing.

— 8 —

This 'eyeball' fixture is made to hold various R lamps, as well as PAR lamps. It swivels in all directions.

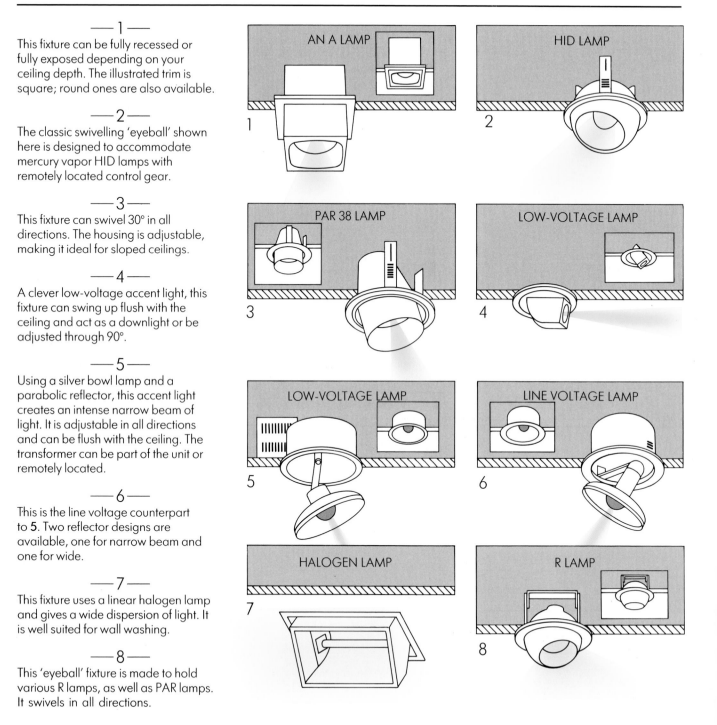

1 — AN A LAMP

2 — HID LAMP

3 — PAR 38 LAMP

4 — LOW-VOLTAGE LAMP

5 — LOW-VOLTAGE LAMP

6 — LINE VOLTAGE LAMP

7 — HALOGEN LAMP

8 — R LAMP

W·A·L·L L·I·G·H·T·I·N·G

The lights that are designed to illuminate walls have been named according to three basic techniques of wall lighting.

Wall washing Fixtures known as wall washers are intended to produce an even 'wash' of light that will illuminate an entire wall. All reputable manufacturers publish recommended spacing dimensions for their wall washers. Placing them closer to a wall than recommended results in scalloped patterns of light. Trying to wash glossy wall surfaces results in 'hot spots' of glare emerging from the light sources.

Accent lighting The fixtures generally referred to as accent lights are used to highlight paintings and objects. Accent units employ PAR or low-voltage lamps, which come in a variety of fixed beam spreads. The apparatus holding the lamp can be adjusted, usually to a maximum of 35° from vertical and 358° in rotation. You cannot accurately determine the correct angle and lamp until you know the size and precise position of the object to be lit.

Graze lighting This system is usually built into the ceiling as an architectural detail. The light sources should be within 305mm (12in) of the wall. The light emphasizes the top of the wall, and even illumination is achieved by using many lamps, usually R lamps, placed closely together. Brushing a wall with light in this way is especially effective when it is used to exaggerate the textural interest of rough surfaces.

The stone chimney over the fireplace is an eye-catching architectural feature of the room pictured above. Several lamps placed not far apart, recessed into the ceiling, are graze lighting the chimney wall, bringing out still further the already bold statement made by the uneven stone.

105

— 1 —

Manufacturers give recommendations for smooth wall washing based on a fixture's distance from the wall and on the distance between fixtures. Here typical data for a 150-watt A lamp system are given, both in imperial and in metric measurements.

These data are valid whenever the fixtures' distance from the wall and from each other are the same (a good rule of thumb) – in this case 910mm or 3ft apart. Whereas if you just have a single unit, the footcandle levels on either side of the fixture fall off rapidly, you can see how multiple units fill the space to create a smooth and even wash.

These data are based on a ceiling 3m (10ft) high. For higher ceilings you would place your units further from the wall, to maintain the best illumination at typical viewing height – approximately 1.5m (5ft).

— 2 —

This double wall washer does what its name implies: it effectively lights both walls in a narrow passage, and also directs some light downward.

— 3 —

This is a corner wall washer, and again its function is obvious from its name. It is used to create a smooth continuum of light between two adjoining walls.

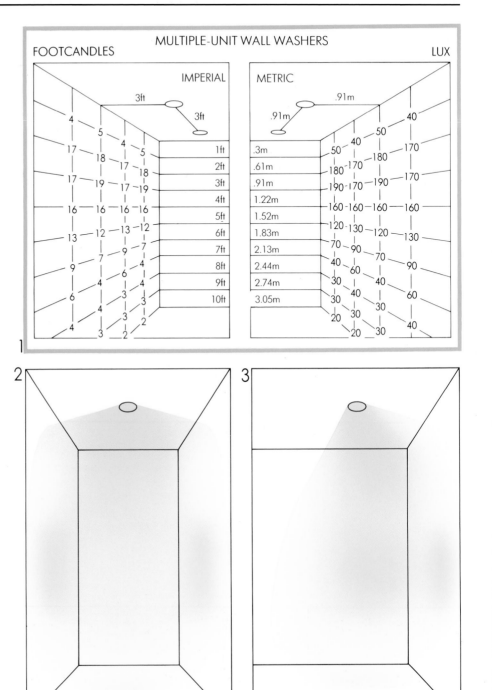

—4—

An accent light using miniaturized low-voltage technology has the advantage of taking up little ceiling depth and of requiring a small ceiling opening. Accent units on line voltage employ PAR lamps and need greater ceiling depth and larger openings.

—5—

This washer incorporates a spread lens placed near the aperture and uses the efficient PAR lamp. It provides a more precise cut-off of spill light from the sides and bottom than **6**.

—6—

This is a typical, open-aperture wall washer. It uses a frosted A lamp and provides the most even wall illumination of all the fixtures illustrated. In all wall washers the light level falls off most rapidly on the bottom third of the wall.

—7—

The framing projector is a specialized accent light. By incorporating focusing lenses and adjustable shutters, the unit enables you to frame a painting precisely.

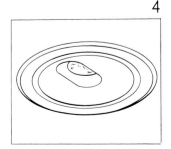

4

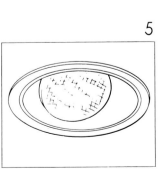

5

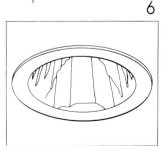

6

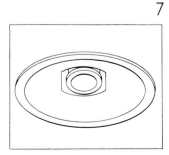

7

T·R·A·C·K

Track was introduced in the 1950s and was immediately a huge success, answering any number of previously expensive or insoluble problems. Mainly, track allows you to introduce your electric current at any point and continue it anywhere you want, with a minimum amount of structural damage and a maximum degree of flexibility.

There are disadvantages to track. For instance, a fixture accommodating a PAR 38 can hang down 305mm (12in), which is imposing in a room of average height. Because the fixtures are always exposed, track has to be considered as a decorative design element. But the advantage of extreme flexibility often outweighs styling – shortly after its introduction every manufacturer was offering his line of track.

This leads to another drawback, or frustration. All track systems are different and the fixtures for one company's track do not fit that of another's. There are now companies

that make fixtures but not track and they offer an adaptable line. And there are also specialized outfits, which will adapt fixtures for a price. In any case, all the little bits that go into forming a complete system can be complex and are not interchangeable. On the other hand, many manufacturers and distributors will assist you with involved track designs.

The recent introduction of low-voltage lighting (see page 84) has stimulated the track companies to release all manner of fixtures. With a remotely located transformer a low-voltage fixture can be as small as 51mm (2in), replacing line voltage lamps that need 305mm (12in).

Track can be recessed, ceiling-mounted, suspended, wall-mounted, or built as a structure secured to the floor. There are multiple-circuit tracks with up to four separately activated and controlled lines. All in all, the flexibility of track often makes it the appropriate solution to a lighting problem.

(see page 84)

TYPICAL TRACK PROFILE

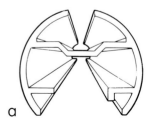

a

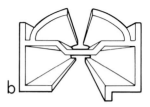

b

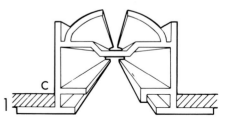

c

1

A SELECTION OF TRACK FIXTURES

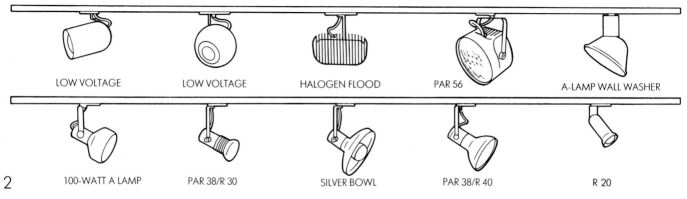

LOW VOLTAGE   LOW VOLTAGE   HALOGEN FLOOD   PAR 56   A-LAMP WALL WASHER

100-WATT A LAMP   PAR 38/R 30   SILVER BOWL   PAR 38/R 40   R 20

2

—1—

The first two of these three typical track styles (shown in cross-section) can be surface-mounted or suspended.
(**a**) Tubular or round track is available in diameters of 50, 70, 90, 100, 200mm (2, $2\frac{3}{4}$, $3\frac{1}{2}$, 4, 8in).
(**b**) Rectangular track has fewer variations in size; it is usually around 35mm ($1\frac{1}{2}$in) wide and 25mm (1in) deep.
(**c**) The least intrusive track is this recessed or flush-mounted one. Semi-recessed models are also available from some makers.

—2—

The two lines of fixtures shown here hold almost every type of lamp. Many manufacturers produce complete ranges of fixtures – as you can see, the variation in design is enormous.

—3—

A luminous architectural element, this tubular track holds many tiny, low-voltage lamps.

—4—

This track kit complete with flex and switch can be mounted anywhere you wish, while the fixtures can be interchanged and their focus altered.

—5—

Made for linear metal halide HID lamps (see p.94), this fixture contains the control gear and has a protective glass to absorb ultraviolet wave-lengths. It could make a most effective wall washer.

—6—

This is a wall washer, designed to hold linear fluorescent tubes. The baffle shields the lamps when viewed from the end of the fixture.

UNUSUAL TRACK FIXTURES

3

4

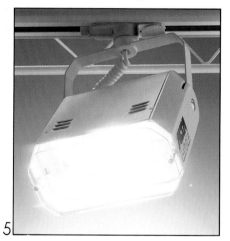
5

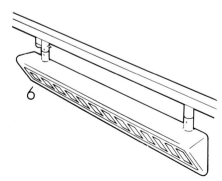
6

—MODULAR TRACK—

Shown here is a modular system by Artemide called 'Anton Barra'. The flexibility of such track-inspired designs is evident.

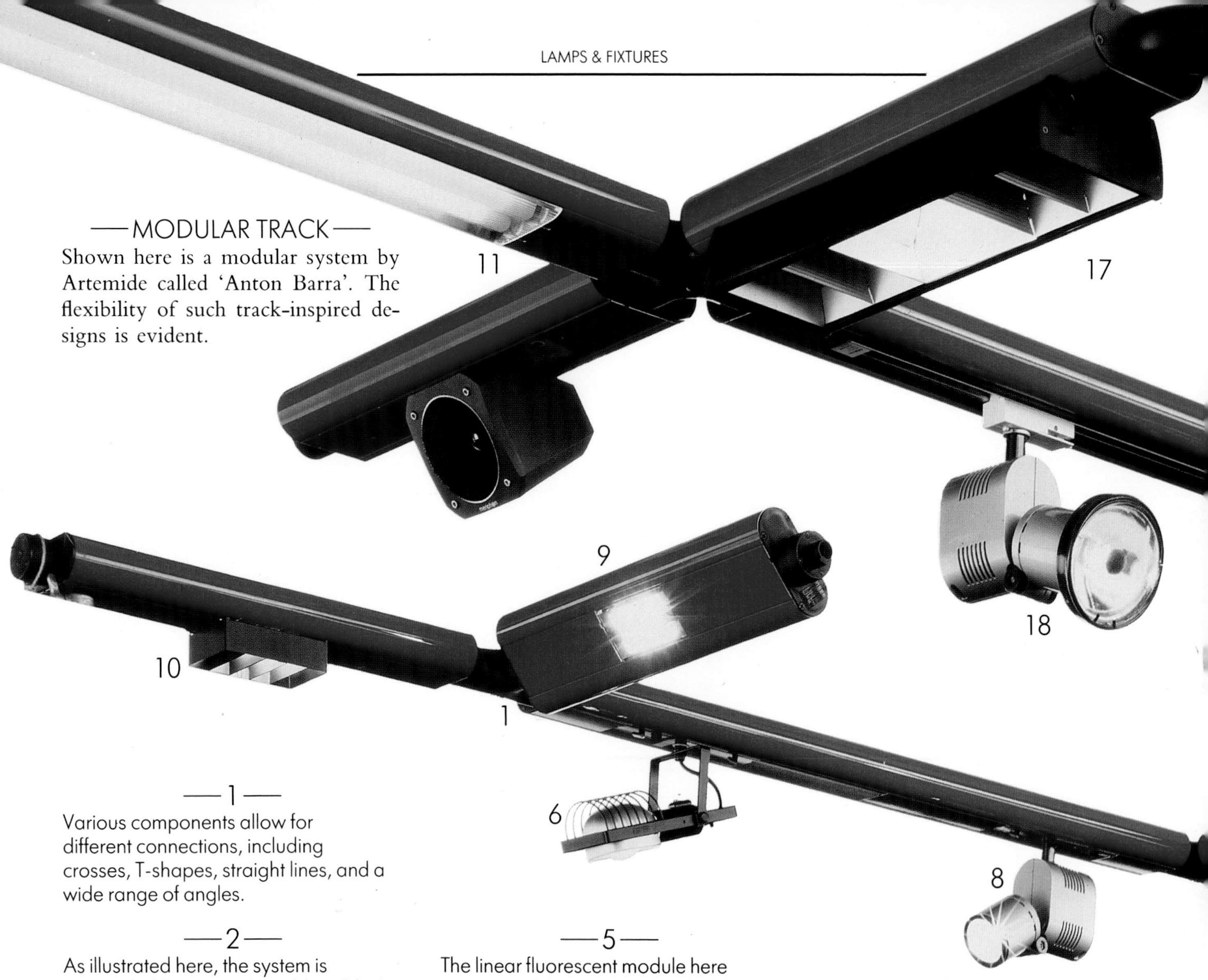

11

17

9

18

10

1

6

8

—1—

Various components allow for different connections, including crosses, T-shapes, straight lines, and a wide range of angles.

—2—

As illustrated here, the system is suspended from an adjustable cable. It can also be surface-mounted.

—3—

The track module is capable of accepting many different fixtures.

—4—

This T-shaped or three-way connector has a linear tungsten halogen fixture attached to it.

—5—

The linear fluorescent module here contains a 20-watt 26mm (1in) tube and a diffusing lens.

—6—

Artemide's standard 'Sintesi' fitting uses an A lamp.

—7—

A 500-watt incandescent dimmer could be useful if placed on a module within your reach.

—8—

This low-voltage fixture with an integral transformer takes a 50-watt, 12-volt reflector lamp, 50mm (2in) in diameter.

—9—

The linear tungsten halogen fixture here is on a rotating module.

—13—
The same fixture as **12**, this one has a pebbled reflector accessory, that you use with a silver bowl lamp to achieve a solft-edged accent light.

—14—
This linear fluorescent module takes a lamp of 40 watts, 26mm (1in) in diameter.

—15—
This parabolic louvre for **14** shields the lamp and distributes the light more efficiently.

—16—
This low-voltage module has an integrated, concealed transformer. The lamp can be either a 20- or 50-watt, 12-volt halogen capsule with a G4 base.

—17—
This parabolic louvre for the linear fluorescent module **5** causes a more efficient distribution of light.

—10—
This louvre for **9** is deep enough to provide adequate lamp shielding, even though the lamp is close to the surface.

—11—
This two-lamp linear fluorescent has a diffusing lens top and bottom that distributes light both up and down.

—12—
A simple and straightforward fixture this is designed to hold either an R or a PAR lamp up to 150 watts.

—18—
This low-voltage PAR 36 fixture is supplied with its own integral, concealed transformer.

S·U·R·F·A·C·E F·I·X·T·U·R·E·S

WALL- OR CEILING-
—MOUNTED—

Almost all types of fixtures designed to be recessed are also available surface-mounted; and it is surface-mounted fixtures that are most commonly displayed in lighting shops.

They are more expensive than recessed fixtures, because you are paying for the design of the fixture as well as for the suitability of its light. However, should you move, it is possible to take surface-mounted fixtures with you.

Fixtures usually come in a limited number of finishes, most often black, white, silver (chrome), and gold (brass). A number of manufacturers offer other colors on special order; there are also specialized shops that will paint fixtures to suit your needs, using a special heat-resistant paint.

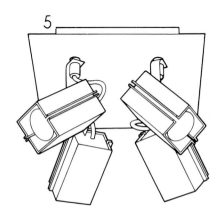

1

2

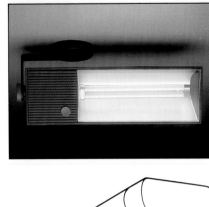

4

5

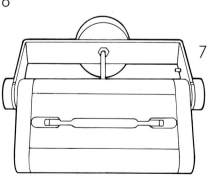

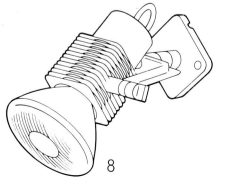

—1—

These wall washers can hold either 100-watt frosted A lamps or 9-watt SL lamps; they produce a smooth, low-intensity wash of light. An 11-watt, PL model is also available.

—2—

140mm ($5\frac{1}{2}$in) in diameter, this rotating unit is held in place by a magnet and can be mounted anywhere, on a wall, a ceiling, or under a shelf. It uses a 60-watt R 20 lamp, and is available with an anti-glare louvre.

—3—

This is an elegant fixture for an 11-watt PL lamp, which can be mounted vertically or horizontally.

—4—

This extruded aluminium tube is made in varying lengths to accommodate linear fluorescent tubes. It can be mounted in any orientation, and the tube rotates.

—5—

Available in two- or four-head configurations, this low-voltage fitting has an integral transformer and uses 12-volt 50-watt reflector lamps.

—6—

This compact unit (115mm or $4\frac{1}{2}$in deep) is designed as a wall washer for a linear fluorescent lamp.

—7—

Using a 200- or 300-watt linear halogen lamp, this fixture can be used on a ceiling for wall washing or on a wall for indirect lighting.

—8—

This simple lampholder taking a PAR 38 is adjustable in all directions, and can be used as an accent light.

PORTABLE FIXTURES

The fixtures on this page all plug into wall sockets, so they allow you to provide an accent of light almost anywhere you like. And, of course, you can also alter the lighting in your room by moving them about. With the development of low-voltage lamps, some fixtures are even small enough to be hidden behind planters or similar objects.

To make your line voltage portable lamps even more flexible, you can attach in-line dimmers to them (see pages 130–31). And the increasing popularity of low-voltage units undoubtedly means that in-line dimmers will soon be available for them as well.

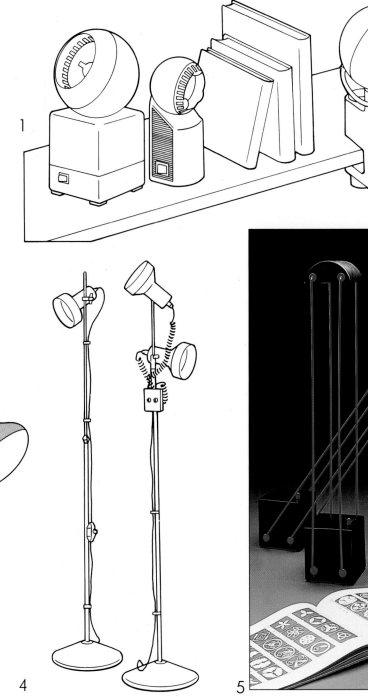

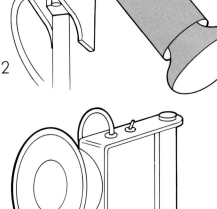

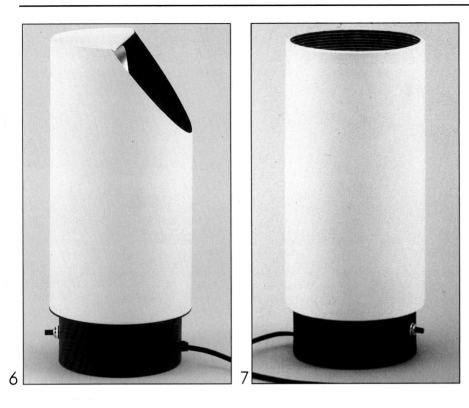

6

7

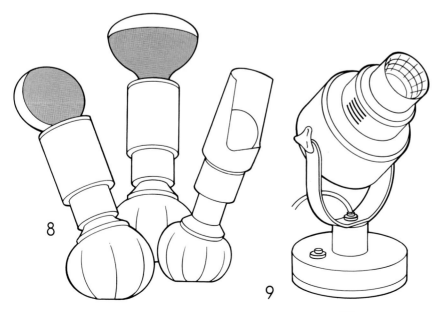

8

9

—1—

These fixtures – two low-voltage and one line voltage (right) – are about 140mm (5$\frac{1}{2}$in) high. Held by a magnet, the heads can rotate on the base.

—2—

This basic clamp-on fixture is capable of accepting a wide range of line voltage display spots.

—3—

Only 160mm (6in) tall, this fixture has an integral transformer and uses a 12-volt 20-watt halogen lamp within a fixed reflector.

—4—

These easily portable accent lights are very flexible. They slide up and down the stem, and are adjustable sideways.

—5—

Using a 100-watt, 12-volt lamp, this adjustable fixture is an intense task light.

—6—

A built-in reflector converts this uplight can to a wall washer. This is an effective way of emphasizing texture.

—7—

This is the classic uplight 'can'. About 330mm (13in) tall, it takes an R or PAR 38 lamp of 150 watts.

—8—

A bean bag base allows this lamp to be pointed in many directions. The little fixture, only 200mm (8in) tall, accepts a variety of lamps and accessories.

—9—

The manufacturer of this track fixture offers a weighted base so that the fixture can be made portable. It accepts 12-volt 50-watt reflector lamps and has an integral transformer.

P·E·N·D·A·N·T L·I·G·H·T·S

Any hanging fixture comes into the category familiarly known as pendants. A pendant light can be as simple as merely a bare lamp suspended on an electrical cable, or it can be as ornate and elaborate as a chandelier in Versailles. The choice is yours.

Pendants are suspended either by thin cables or by metal stems; both support the lamp housing and the electrical cable, and both are adjustable. Their final position is often a compromise: the ideal height for the intensity and spread of light may not be compatible with your normal viewing angle, where the lamp should be shielded to prevent glare. For example, a pendant above a dining-room table should be low enough to cast a pool of light on the table, but high enough not to block dinner guests' views of each other. Many pendant fixtures now have spring-loaded or counterweight devices, allowing height adjustment.

1

2

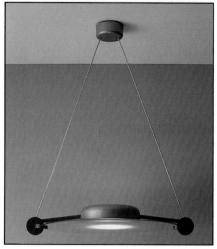

3

— 1 —

A built-in pulley system permits the height of this pendant to be adjusted easily. The fixture uses either 20- or 50-watt halogen capsules and the transformer is integral.

— 2 —

This stem-mounted linear pendant is unique. It has linear halogen lamps mounted above so that indirect light can be bounced off the ceiling, while low-voltage reflector lamps below provide accent lighting.

— 3 —

This distinctive pendant uses two 100-watt A lamps. The circular piece of glass has a frosted center, which diffuses the light.

— 4 —

The shades of these pendants are made of heat-resistant synthetic material, which can be cut to a desired shape and colored. The pendants take silver bowl lamps, so there is a balance between diffused up- and downlight. They are available with counterweights, for height adjustment.

— 5 —

The outward light is diffused by an opal glass cylinder, around which floats a design of stepped aluminium discs. Either a 100-watt A lamp or a 25-watt SL will fit this pendant.

— 6 —

This simple fixture has an acrylic tube that assumes the shape of its PL lamp. The tube serves to diffuse the light and make the essentially bare lamp less glaring. The control gear is in the linear ceiling canopy.

4

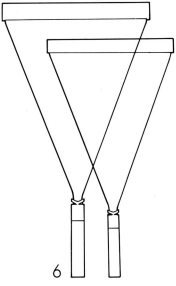

5

6

W·A·L·L L·I·G·H·T·S

Manufacturers hardly ever publish any photometric data for wall lights, because people usually choose them for their decorative value rather than for the quality of their light. In fact the illumination they provide can be useful as well as attractive, provided that you make your choice wisely.

Fixtures that direct most of their light upward, for indirect lighting, are the most practical if you want general soft illumination. Those relying on some sort of diffuser are of less practical value, though more interesting as luminous objects. Bear in mind that if the brightness of this second group is not carefully considered, contrast between fixtures and the wall can be overwhelming, especially if the fixtures are pale and the wall is dark. Before you decide to buy any wall lights, it makes sense to see what they look like when they are turned on.

1

2

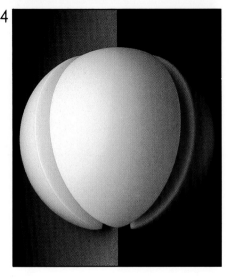

3

4

5

7

6

—1—

This beautifully crafted fixture is made of steel and glass. The perforated steel shields a single-ended halogen lamp and reflects the light on to the wall, while the edges of the glass appear to be lit from within.

—2—

This small 'nightlight', which takes a 15-watt lamp, plugs directly into a socket. It has a built-in photo-electric cell so that it turns itself on and off automatically, according to a pre-set pattern.

—3—

This classic wall sconce throws a wide, smooth light pattern upwards; the resulting light is both indirect and atmospheric.

—4—

A series of opal glass spheres mounted on a corner of an outside wall make for interesting lighting possibilities. The fitting uses a 100-watt A lamp or an 18-watt SL lamp.

—5—

Slender metal rods attach the head of this fitting to its wall canopy. It uses a linear halogen lamp and throws a wash of light on to the ceiling and upper part of a wall.

—6—

Stained-glass techniques much used in the Art Deco period are enjoying a renewed popularity. This type of fixture casts little useful light: it is really just an object of luminal art.

—7—

A wash of uplight is cast by this fixture, which employs a linear halogen lamp. The unit is made of aluminium, and it has a floor-standing counterpart.

T·A·B·L·E L·I·G·H·T·S

In the early days of electric lighting, the portable light that sat on a table was the most common source of illumination. This table light or lamp is just as popular today, especially in spaces where there is some feeling of 'period' design.

Table lamps traditionally consist of a lampholder with a conical shade that hides the lamp and diffuses the light. The shape determines the spread of light. If the shades are too cylindrical, they funnel the light into useless narrow beams – consider their proportion and what they do with the light before you buy. Fixtures with translucent shades allow light to spread horizontally, like daylight. Shades with open tops direct light upwards to bounce off the ceiling.

The ideal table lamp has two light sources, one higher up, for bouncing light off the ceiling, and one lower down, for tasks and for throwing direct light on to surfaces. Most often, however, there is only one centrally placed lamp. In all cases, as with their floor-standing cousins, you should position table lights so that you cannot see into the shade from above while standing or from below while sitting.

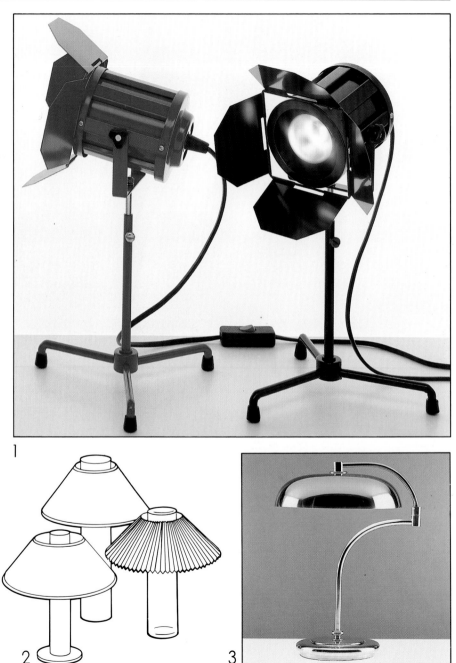

1

2

3

120

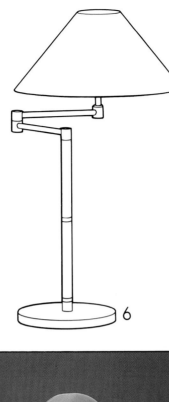

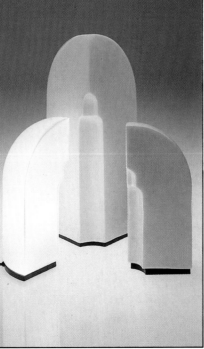

—1—

This is an example of a miniature theatrical fitting adapted for a table lamp. Its height is adjustable up to 38cm (15in). A 40-watt R lamp gives a directional light.

—2—

A pleated linen shade diffuses more light than a smooth one, but in both types of lamp the wide, conical shape allows for good downward light distribution. The brass stem on the left has a unique touch switch for three intensities of light from a 150-watt A lamp.

—3—

In this brass fitting, which takes an A lamp, all light is directed downwards. The shade pivots, allowing some degree of flexibility.

—4—

This elegant table light takes a low-wattage A lamp, giving off soft ambient light.

—5—

This marble table lamp by Flos must be considered more of a luminous sculpture than a practical fixture.

—6—

This miniature version of a floor lamp is interesting, because the swivel joints allow flexible positioning.

—7—

A series of beautiful luminous shapes, these white opal glass lamps give off a soft, even, atmospheric light.

4

6

5

7

T·A·S·K L·I·G·H·T·S

A task light should provide an even area of light at an intensity suited to the difficulty of the task. This might be anywhere between 50 and 200 fc. The lamp head should be adjustable, so that you can direct the light towards the task.

As well as the desktop units shown here, many pendant fixtures are obtainable that incorporate linear fluorescent lamps. These distribute light over a large area and their intensity is controlled by their height from the work surface. A wide selection of under-shelf task lights is available as well.

If you choose a task light that uses low-voltage lamps, take care that the reflector provides even light with no 'hot' or 'dead' spots.

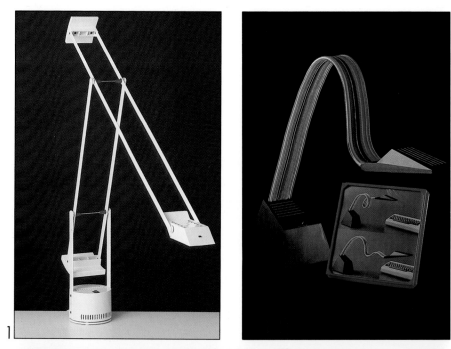

1

2

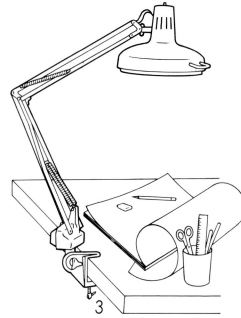

3

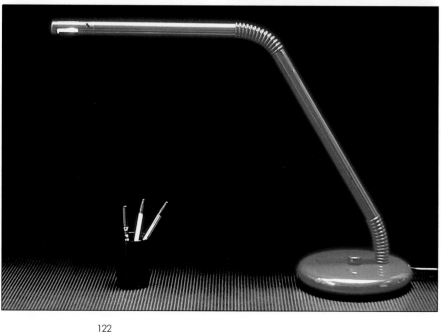

4

—1—

The poised elegance of Artemide's 'Tizio' lamp is already a legend. The fitting's counterbalanced arms carry the 12-volt current to the 55-watt lamp. A two-position switch is incorporated into the base, which also houses the transformer.

—2—

This unusual, low-voltage fixture has a flexible 'ribbon' arm, while its base holds the transformer.

—3—

This is the classic architect's lamp. The best incorporate both an A lamp and a circular fluorescent lamp. Accessories allow for wall or desk attachment, and spring-loaded arms permit almost limitless adjustment.

—4—

Thin and streamlined, this 12-volt, 50-watt task light has its transformer in the base, which also holds a built-in dimmer.

—5—

The narrow linear design of this fixture complements the PL lamp it uses. The necessary control gear is built into the clamp-on base.

—6—

This fixture uses an A lamp and has a reflector on the top to direct light downward. Weighted base or clamp-on models are available.

—7—

This task light has a precise and narrow beam. It takes a 12-volt, 5-watt lamp, and its transformer is the weighted base. The flexible stem is designed to slip out of the base and fit directly into the cigarette lighter of a car.

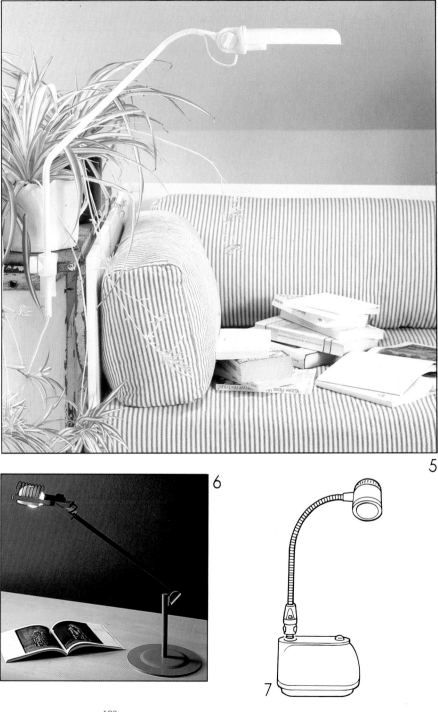

5

6

7

F·L·O·O·R L·I·G·H·T·S

Together with table lamps, floor-standing lamps often provide the majority of the illumination in rooms where additional wall or ceiling wiring is considered to be impractical.

Floor lamps that direct most of their light upwards provide soft, indirect, ambient light and should have a smooth distribution. As most floor lights are moveable, they have the advantage that you can redirect light to different areas as needed. Remember that electric cords should not trail, and even when put under rugs they can be a fire risk.

Because of the huge selection, those illustrated are mostly 'designer' fixtures, rather than the tall cousins of the classic table lamps shown on pages 120–21.

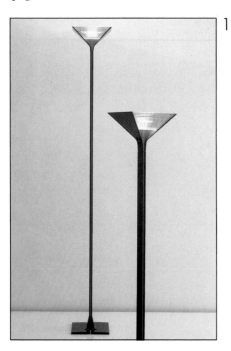

1

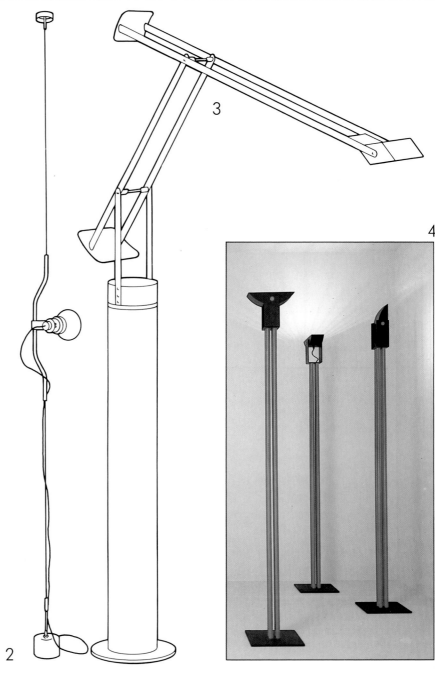

2

3

4

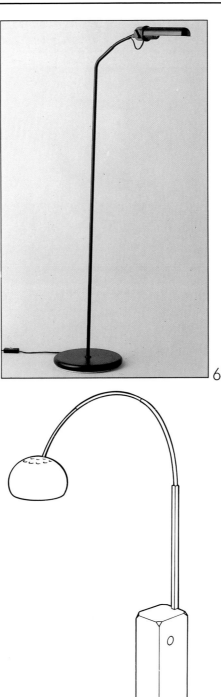

—1—

The prismatic glass sides of this uplighter distribute a portion of its light horizontally. A dimmer is built into the light, which uses a linear halogen lamp.

—2—

A cable suspended from ceiling to floor forms a track along which you can slide the lampholder. This flexible fixture can accommodate a PAR 38, which could be used as an accent light.

—3—

Here is the 'Tizio' lamp (see 1, p. 122) with a floor base. Its added height makes it possible to use for bouncing indirect light off the ceiling.

—4—

The head of this fixture, which takes a linear halogen lamp, can be adjusted to wash a wall or uplight a ceiling.

—5—

The glass bowl of this austere and delicate lamp comes in various colors, which give off a glow; yet most of the light from the halogen lamp is directed upwards. You can also buy a wall-mounted version.

—6—

This fixture, which takes a PL lamp and has integral control gear, makes a practical reading light. The rotating head allows you to focus the light as you wish.

—7—

This standing lamp is as tall as an average man. It casts a wide distribution of light downwards.

E·X·T·E·R·I·O·R L·I·G·H·T·S

In recent years a great many innovative fixtures for outdoor use have been introduced.

Many of the newer ones take advantage of the long life and energy-efficiency of compact fluorescent and HID lamps.

Exterior fittings need to be constructed of good-quality, weatherproof materials and the electrical parts must be protected from the elements. Before you choose, think about whether a fixture needs to be secured in the ground (which requires buried wiring), mounted on a wall, or secured to solid flooring. And, of course, make sure that any fixture you buy has been approved for exterior use.

2

4

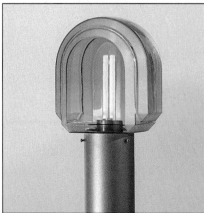

3

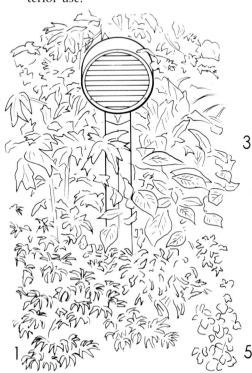

1

5

— 1 —

This handsome fixture is available in several colors, takes an A lamp, and comes with a clear or prismatic lens.

— 2 —

The linear halogen lamp used by this floodlight is capable of illuminating the side of a house.

— 3 —

This bollard is available with a brown-tinted or clear glass cover. A low-level light is cast by the 13-watt PL lamp.

— 4 —

This outdoor accent light holds PAR lamps. The heads swivel, allowing the light to be focused.

— 5 —

Portable, inexpensive, and not dazzlingly bright, Christmas tree lights add sparkle all year round.

— 6 —

Available in heights of 720 or 400mm (2ft 4in or 1ft 4in), the opal glass of this bollard diffuses the light of either an A or an SL lamp.

— 7 —

These tiny, low-voltage strings of light are encased in weatherproof plastic. They allow you to light stairs, handrails, or simply to put a line or curve of light anywhere you like.

— 8 —

Called 'step' lights, these fixtures are recessed into walls or the risers of stairs. They hold A or PL lamps and come with lenses or louvres.

— 9 —

This unobtrusive wall-mounted fixture directs light downwards and can take either A, PL, or HID lamps

C·O·N·T·R·O·L·S

Many physical devices can reshape, redirect, and otherwise redefine the characteristics of a light source. Dimmers, which control the quantity of light, are discussed on pages 130 and 131.

Reflectors Fixtures that hold omni-directional lamps, like A and fluorescent, need some sort of reflector to redirect the normally unusable upward light downwards.

In the early days, reflectors were often mirrors but today most are made of polished aluminium. The finish of such reflectors is usually silver, often referred to as clear. Many fixtures, however, are offered with gold-colored reflectors. This decreases the light output by approximately 10 per cent, while also influencing the color of the light,

adding 'warmth'. Gold reflectors are mostly used to help normally cool lamps, such as HID and fluorescent, appear more like conventional incandescent sources.

Louvres A louvre is a gridlike screen. Its main function is to shield a lamp from view within the 45° cut-off zone (see page 100). Thus any fitting that is in your normal sight-line, and where the lamp is near the fixture's opening, is a candidate for a louvre (sometimes called an anti-dazzle screen). This includes linear fluorescent fixtures and a great many of the new low-voltage spotlights where the lamp is not recessed into the fixture.

The most common type of louvre is called an egg-crate, composed of many square cells usually 13mm ×

13mm ($\frac{1}{2}$in × $\frac{1}{2}$in). Normally white or black, louvres are available in a variety of materials, such as aluminium and plastic. Some can re-aim light in a direction other than downward. Such a louvre on a linear fluorescent fitting might be used in a kitchen, for example, to redirect light towards cabinets or shelves.

Lenses Those lenses that cover a fixture's aperture will of course hide the lamp, but they do not make it invisible as a louvre does. Instead a lens spreads the brightness of a lamp over a larger area, with the effect of reducing glare. Lenses are made in many styles to direct light in various patterns, and are either of glass or of various plastics. (Try and avoid lenses that are made of polystyrene, which yellows with age.)

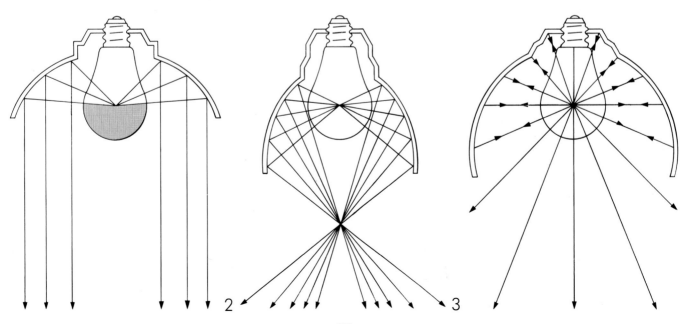

— 1 —

The parabolic reflector shown here theoretically redirects light into a parallel beam. This depends on the light emanating from a precise 'point'. As all filaments are larger than a point, in practice the light is scattered into a cone pattern. Parabolic reflectors are used for many accent lights.

— 2 —

The most frequently used reflectors in downlights are elliptical ones: they take the light from the ideal 'point' mentioned above and redirect it back through a second point.

— 3 —

A reflector based on a circle or sphere takes the light from the 'point' and in theory redirects it straight back through itself, doubling its intensity. Spherical reflectors are most used in projection systems and with linear incandescent tubes.

— 4 —

The Targa series by Concord illustrated here has been designed to accept many types of control devices. (a) This is a framing projector lens attachment. It allows you to shape the beam of light via the shutters – for example, to frame a painting precisely. (b) A fresnel lens accessory softens the light and allows the beam to be focused into spot or flood configurations. (c) This attachment allows you to insert colored glass filters or clear striated ones that spread the light beam along one axis. (d) An egg-crate louvre shields the lamp from view. (e) Commonly called a barn door attachment, this accessory lets you control spill light and allows a degree of beam shaping. (f) Often called a top hat or snoot, this device cuts off spill light and acts as a shield.

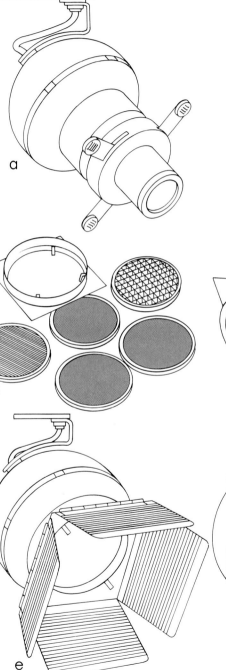

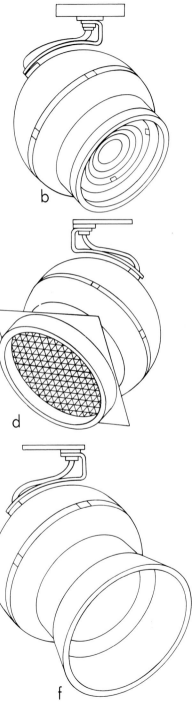

DIMMERS AND SWITCHES

The most common type of dimmer fits into the wall and replaces your existing switch. For such relatively low cost, the rewards are well worth the replacement.

A dimmer allows you to participate in your lighting. It gives you the flexibility to adjust light levels and create different areas of importance or interest. The modern electronic dimmer cuts your electricity consumption and – in the case of tungsten lamps – increases the life of your lamp. Reducing your voltage by 5 per cent will decrease your light output by only 15 per cent, while increasing the lamp life by as much as 80 per cent.

Incandescent lamps The easiest lamps to dim are tungsten and tungsten halogen, for which you can buy wall dimmers that will accommodate loads up to 2000 watts. Dimming incandescent lamps lowers their Kelvin temperature (see page 91), shifting them to the warmer yellow and amber colors; this imitates candlelight and enhances atmosphere.

Low-voltage lamps are also easily dimmed, though they do need a special low-voltage dimmer.

Fluorescent lamps Since the output of linear fluorescent lamps is related to their length (see page 90), it is helpful to be able to dim them. (The more recent compact fluorescents, on the other hand, are not dimmable.) A special ballast is usually required, but electronic wizardry is fast reducing the size and cost of such ballasts to a practical level. And you can now buy wall-mounted dimmers that look like incandescent dimmers. Dimming fluorescent lamps does not dramatically alter their color temperature, another difference between fluorescent and incandescent lamps.

HID lamps Because these were initially developed for industry, dimming was not an initial consideration. But now even HID lamps are having dimmers developed for them.

——CONTROL SENSORS——

Dimming systems have benefited from innovations relating to security control. You can buy motion detectors based on radar, originally developed to detect burglars, but now able to sense your presence and turn on the lights for you even before you enter the room. There are infrared sensors that analyse heat patterns to decide whether to turn on your lights (or for that matter any electric device). Sonic sensors decipher sound wave formations. And all these technologies could be feeding information to a computer.

——COMPUTER CONTROL——

The computer marvels are still too expensive and sophisticated for most homes. But remote devices that send signals to your existing wiring are not. Small receivers like the remote control on a television are activated by infrared signals or sound waves: you could have a small box – about the size of a little radio – by your bed, and it could turn on and off, or dim, the lights in your nursery, hall, or kitchen – or even activate your coffee maker, toaster, or stereo.

—1—

This a wall-mounted dimmer, operated by a sliding control.

—2—

This type of dimmer works by what is known as a touch control. By tapping the center plate you can switch on or dim the lights.

—3—

Another wall dimmer, this one has a rotary control.

—4—

There is a sliding control on this wall dimmer, as well as a rocker switch used to maintain a preset light level.

—5—

Illustrated are four 'in-line' dimmers of the type that are attached to the cords of table lamps and other portable fixtures. The controls are operated differently, but all allow incandescent lamps of up to 300 watts to be dimmed.

—6—

This is an example of a time delay switch. An energy-saving device, it keeps lights on for a predetermined amount of time, up to several minutes.

—7—

The mechanical timer illustrated here is plugged into a wall socket, with a lamp plugged into it. The light can then be turned on and off automatically several times in a 24-hour period.

—8—

A photo-electric cell activates this wall-mounted switch. A slide mechanism allows the activation time to be altered, while a small neon light indicates when the device is on.

—9—

The photo-electric cell shown here is weatherproof and suitable for outdoor use. For example, it can activate porch lights at dusk, turning them off again at dawn.

—10—

This type of timer replaces a wall switch, controlling the same number of lights that there were on the switch. The timer can be programmed to turn lights on and off at a given time.

—11—

This hand-held controller uses infrared signals, in conjunction with sending and receiving modules and with existing wiring. It is capable of controlling as many as sixteen lighting or electrical devices.

—12—

This remote control uses a radio frequency to activate various modules. Signals are sent over existing wiring, and the control can either be used manually or else specifically programmed to activate electrical circuits at predetermined times.

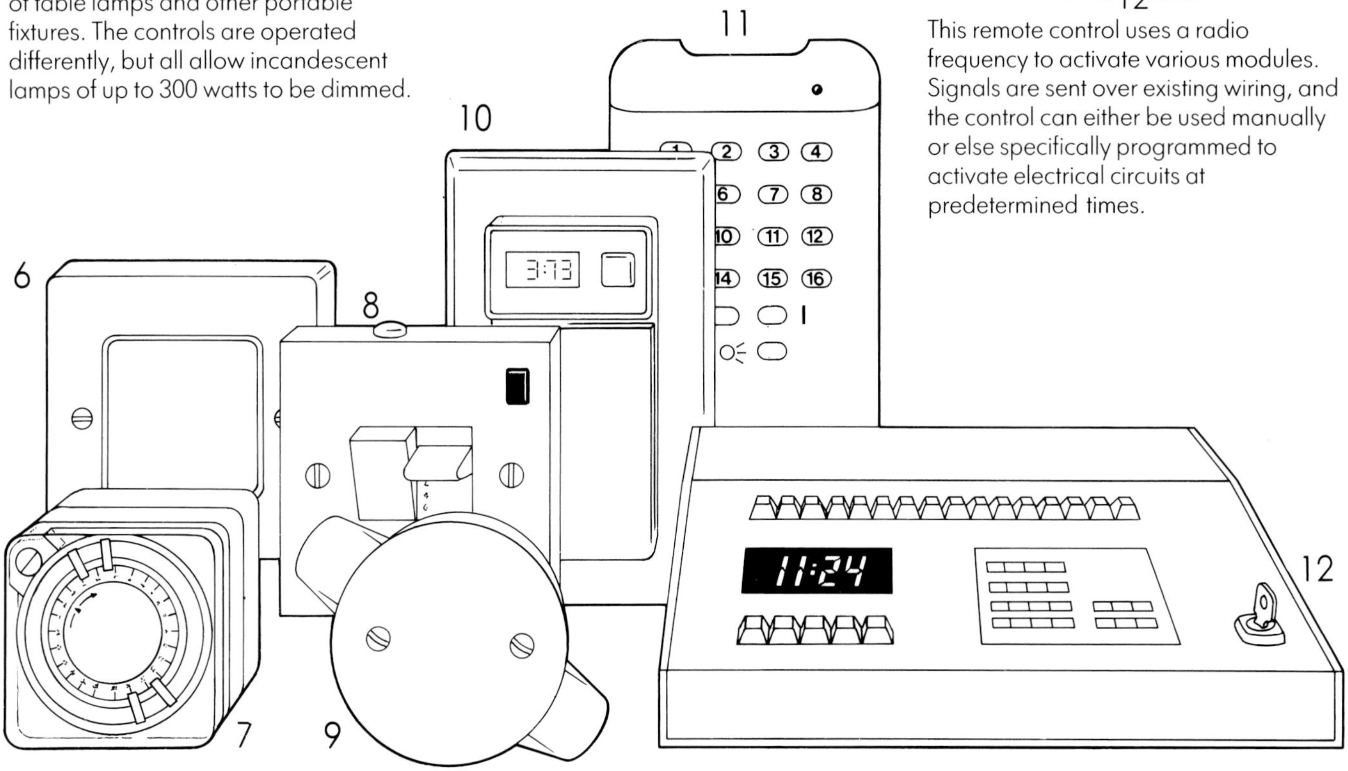

MAINTENANCE

Most people pay very little attention to the upkeep of their lighting system. At best they change burned-out lamps immediately and use the correct type of lamp in replacement. Since producing light is basically energy-inefficient, more maintenance than this is necessary to make the most of what you have.

Maintenance Because lamps produce heat, they set up convection currents in the air, and the air is full of dust and dirt. Fixtures need to be cleaned regularly, especially those with reflectors and/or lenses. A dirty lens or reflector can easily reduce the light output by 50 per cent. And you can guarantee that any dust that does not settle on your fixture will be deposited next to it: this accounts for the soot-like marks you often see near light fixtures.

Most lenses and reflectors can be cleaned with mild soap and water, after they have been taken to pieces. There are some exceptions to this. Any reflectors that are specular (mirror-like), whether silver, gold or black, need special care. The precise reflective quality of the polished metal of these reflectors is easily ruined with fingerprints. Mirror-like finishes on louvres are equally difficult to clean, and are best served by judicious dusting.

Water can play havoc with any light fixture, especially if in contact with the socket or reflector. Any fittings that have been inadvertently exposed to moisture should be checked for the condition of the seals, the socket, and the reflector.

Storage Because every fixture is designed around a particular lamp, it is important that each time a lamp is changed, the correct one is used to replace it. A good idea is to have on hand extra lamps of all the types you use, and keep them in one place. While a stock of lamps can require a considerable initial financial outlay, the price of lamps rarely comes down, so consider buying in bulk an investment.

The cost of making lamps is mere pennies, and their retail value depends largely on the volume sold of any particular lamp. Because of this, purchasing lamps by the case can work out considerably less expensive than buying them individually. A case of 100-watt A lamps may hold between 100 and 120 pieces, whereas a case of low-voltage or linear halogen lamps contains between 6 and 24 pieces, and a case of fluorescent lamps will have between 12 and 30 pieces. PAR lamps are normally packed in dozens, and R lamps come 24 to a case.

FOOTCANDLE LEVELS

This chart is intended to help you understand footcandles (fc), by listing some types of light with which you are familiar and translating them into fc. Recommended fc levels are also given for people of various ages (your eyes' ability to adapt to poor lighting conditions decreases with age) in several ordinary domestic circumstances. If your task demands speed or accuracy, you need the number of fc recommended for the age bracket above your own. If it demands speed and accuracy, you may need fc for two age brackets above your own.

SOME TYPICAL FC LEVELS

Bright, sunny day	5000–10,000
Dull, cloudy day	200–1000
Shop window display	100–500
100-watt architect's lamp, 500mm (1ft 8in) from work surface	150
Single candle flame	1

SOME RECOMMENDED FC LEVELS

	UNDER 40	40–55	OVER 55
Casual reading or writing	20	30	50
Prolonged or difficult reading or writing	50	75	100
Non-critical kitchen task	20	30	50
Critical kitchen task	50	75	100
Fine, detailed sewing	100	150	200
Shaving, making up etc.	20	30	50
Conversation, relaxation (light levels need not be uniform)	5	7.5	10

U·S·E·F·U·L
I·N·F·O·R·M·A·T·I·O·N

☐ Making a lighting plan

☐ Communicating your lighting needs

☐ Addresses of suppliers and manufacturers of

lighting equipment

☐ Glossary of terms

☐ Index and acknowledgments

M·A·K·I·N·G A L·I·G·H·T·I·N·G P·L·A·N

So far in this book I have tried to make you think about light – what it is, and how it influences your view of things. Now I want to help you use your knowledge to communicate with others. I am not attempting to deal with 'do-it-yourself' installations in this section, or indeed anywhere in this book. The practical nuts and bolts of lighting and electricity are best left to the professional tradesman whose job it is to deal with them: the electrician.

A plan of your lighting scheme, like the one below, serves as a map for the electrician to work from. It is also useful as a record of the work, should there be some dispute. Drawing up such a plan is not as difficult as you might think.

The easiest method is to use a piece of graph paper, where the ruled lines are to scale ($\frac{1}{4}$in is common, meaning that $\frac{1}{4}$in = 1ft). Start by tracing the outlines of your room, indicating the position of all the doors and

A lighting plan, like the one below, should be drawn up in as much detail as possible, but it should not look either cluttered or confusing. For certain details, such as wall-mounted fittings or multiple switches, you will probably find it helpful to do an elevation drawing.

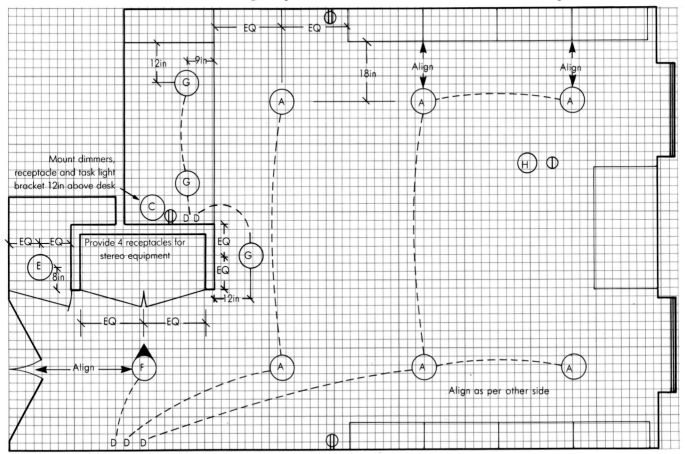

	TYPE	MANUFAC-TURER	CATALOGUE NUMBER	LAMP	ACCESSORIES/COMMENTS	NUMBER REQUIRED
	KEY TO LIGHTING PLAN					
A	Ceiling, surface-mounted	Artemide	Aggregate adjustable spotlight	100-watt A 19 silver bowl	To be fitted with small metal shade	6
C	Wall, surface-mounted	Luxo	LC – 1/A (chrome)	100-watt A 19	Shorten flex so unit plugs in without excess	1
E	Ceiling, surface-mounted, porcelain socket	Various		75-watt A		1
F	Recessed ceiling wall washer	Atlite	A-3 HP A150	150-watt A 21	▲ indicates direction of primary focus	1
G	Recessed ceiling downlight	Atlite	A-1HP A148	75-watt R spot		3
⊕	Black, double receptacle	Leviton	16252 – E			3 plus stereo cabinet
⊕	Single floor receptacle	Hubbel	B-2524			1
D	Single pole 600-watt touch dimmer	Leviton	6606-W			5
H	Floor lamp	Artemide	Tizio with base	55-watt 12-volt (auto lamp)		1

Above is the key to the plan on the left. When you are working out a key or legend of this type, make sure it is on the same piece of paper as the plan, so that there is no danger of it becoming confused with a plan for another room. If lighting is being worked out for many rooms at the same time, be sure to use the symbols to mean the same thing throughout.

windows. Draw in any built-in units and furniture, as they make good reference points for the placement of light fixtures. The symbols you can use to indicate different fixtures are listed in the key on page 135. While there are some standard symbols, the main thing is to be consistent: normally, the letter 'D' is used to mean 'dimmer', but you could just as well use 'X'.

Include in your drawing all the measurements necessary to locate the fixtures accurately. You could give a fixture's distance from a wall, for instance, or say that it should align with the edge of a bookcase, or be equidistant ('EQ' on the plan) between two walls. Curved or dotted lines are usually employed to indicate what lights are controlled by which dimmer or switch. You should make it clear which fixtures and switches are mounted on walls, and next to them on the plan give a measurement as an indication of what the height above finished floor (known as the 'AFF') to the center of the fixture should be.

COMMUNICATING YOUR
——LIGHTING NEEDS——

Depending how involved you become in planning your lighting, you may find that you need to communicate your ideas to a number of different people.

Suppliers The person in the lighting shop where you are buying fixtures, or the retailer who stocks lamps, is your supplier. In all cases, the better informed you are, the more likely it is that you will end up with what you need. Asking for a

'spot' light is like asking for white paint. There are dozens of different types of spotlights. Knowing what you want, and exactly what it is called, will gain you a certain respect and, with luck, a good response from the best suppliers.

Electricians Skilled professional tradesmen, electricians know all there is to know about how to install lighting and wiring.

Do not expect them to be capable of anticipating your lighting needs, or to tell you what fixtures should be used where. Treat them as technical advisers. If you have absorbed the information in this book and have drawn up your own lighting plan, consult your electrician about the electrical requirements such as dimmer capacities, or the right size of wire needed to accommodate the wattages to be used. Electricians should be able to give you helpful advice about the requirements or restrictions of your particular local electrical codes.

Architects and interior designers In many parts of the world, architects consider themselves 'renaissance people', capable of dealing with all elements of a house or its structure. As architecture becomes more specialized, this posture becomes increasingly difficult to maintain. Lighting design has only recently been introduced into the curriculum of an architect's education. As the field is very specialized and expanding rapidly, many are not as well informed as they think, especially when you take into account how much other information they need to keep up with. The result of this shortcoming

is the natural tendency of many architects to use lighting equipment with which they are already familiar and that has worked well for them in the past.

Unfortunately, this approach does not usually lend itself to the most creative or most up-to-date lighting solutions.

If you retain an architect or designer part of whose job includes designing your lighting, you should be sure to question him or her about every room in your house. First talk about qualities of light. Discuss light for particular tasks, the range of moods you want, and how the light will integrate with your color scheme and the design scheme. As our vocabulary is deficient in words to describe light, you should talk about images or make reference to works of art, lighting you have noticed in magazines, in friends' homes, or in restaurants. Once you both know what kind of light you want, the selection process begins – between you, you must decide which of the thousands of available fixtures that give this desired light will be most appropriate for your color and decorative scheme.

Lighting consultants Should you retain the services of a lighting designer, with luck you are hiring someone who has up-to-date information on all equipment. A lighting designer realizes how light shapes and influences your architecture, and should be asking you all the right questions, intended to draw out your views. You now know enough to be rightly suspicious, should this not turn out to be the case.

This is a perspective drawing of the room for which the lighting plan and key were worked out. It is intended to help you visualize the room ad see the planned lighting scheme in action. (Part of the same room is also shown in the photograph on p.65.)

G·L·O·S·S·A·R·Y

This glossary is loosely bsed on ANSI (American National Standards Institute) Z7.1 – 1976, which is the recommended source for definitions about lighting.

Accent lighting Light used to emphasize an object, an area, or to attract attention.

Adaptation The process by which the eye adjusts to a change in light level.

Ambient light *General light*, often *indirect*, or entering a room from an adjacent space.

Baffle An opaque or translucent element used to shield a *lamp* from view or to absorb unwanted light.

Ballast A device used with *HID* and *fluorescent lamps* to establish the circuit conditions necessary to start and operate the *lamp*.

Bare lamp An unshielded light source.

Beam The cone of light emerging from a *luminaire*.

Beam angle The part of the cone of light where the *candlepower* is equal to 50 per cent of maximum.

Blinding glare *Glare* so intense that you cannot see for a short period of time.

Brightness see *Luminance*.

Bulb The glass jacket that gives a *lamp* its shape.

Candela A unit of luminous intensity.

Candlepower Luminous intensity expressed in *candelas*.

Color rendering The effect of a light source on an object's color appearance, when compared with another or a reference source.

Contrast The difference in *luminance* between an object and its background.

Control gear see *Ballast*.

Cut-off angle The angle between the vertical axis and the point where the *bare lamp* is no longer visible.

Dichroic mirror An optical filter that selectively reflects some *wavelengths*, while transmitting others.

Diffuse lighting Light that does not come from one dominant direction.

Diffuser A device to scatter light, primarily in *transmission*.

Diffuse reflection One that appears scattered equally in all directions.

Diffusion The process by which light is scattered, either in *reflection* or *transmission*.

Dimmer A device used to regulate the intensity of light from a *lamp*.

Direct glare *Glare* that is the result of excessive *luminance* in the field of view.

Direct lighting When 90 to 100 per cent of light being emitted is in the direction, usually downwards, of the surface to be lit.

Disabling glare *Glare* that reduces visibility and visual performance.

Discomfort glare Annoying *glare* that often does not reduce visibility and visual performance.

Efficacy The ratio of *lumens* generated to *watts* consumed; an expression of efficiency in *LPW*.

Electric discharge lamp The sort where light is produced by passing an electric current through a gas or vapor.

Electro-luminescence The emission of light when a phosphor is excited by an electro-magnetic field.

Electro-magnetic spectrum A continuum of energy encompassing all *wavelengths*, of which visible light is a 'tiny slice'.

Fiber optics A way of transmitting light through long flexible glass or plastic fibers, using the principle of 'total internal' *reflection*.

Field angle The part of the cone of light where the *candlepower* is equal to 10 per cent of maximum.

Filter A device to change, in *transmission*, the quality of light, affecting magnitude and/or *spectral* make-up.

Fitting see *Luminaire*.

Fixture see *Luminaire*.

Fluorescence The emission of light, only during the absorption of radiation of a different *wavelength*.

Fluorescent lamp A low-pressure mercury discharge *lamp*, producing light through the *fluorescence* of its coating.

Flush-mounted luminaire see *Recessed luminaire*.

Footcandle The unit of *illuminance* used in the USA, expressed in *lumens* per square foot.

General lighting Designed to provide a uniform level throughout an area.

Glare Any *brightness* in your field of view that is greater than what your eye is adapted to.

HID lamps High intensity discharge *lamps*, such as mercury, metal halide, and high-pressure sodium lamps.

Illuminance The density of light on a surface.

Incandescence The emission of light by the thermal excitement of a solid or liquid.

Incandescent filament lamp The sort where light is produced by heating a wire (usually tungsten) to *incandescence* with electricity.

Indirect glare Excessive *brightness* (either *blinding*, *disabling*, or *discomforting*) in your field of view from reflective surfaces.

Indirect lighting When 90 to 100 per cent of light being emitted is sent upwards (and bounced back).

Lamp The general term for a man-made source of light. Often called the 'bulb' by the layman, a lamp may also refer to a complete lighting fixture.

Light Electro-magnetic *radiation* detectable by the eye.

Louvre A series of *baffles*, usually geometric, used to shield a *lamp* from view at certain viewing angles.

LPW *Lumens* per *watt*.

Lumen The unit of light energy.

Luminaire A complete lighting unit, including lampholder, power connection, and any internal devices such as *reflectors*; inaccurately called a fitting, a fixture, a light, or a *lamp*.

Luminance The luminous intensity of any visible surface, perceived brightness.

Lux The unit of *illuminance*, expressed in *lumens* per square metre. Used everywhere except in the USA.

Plenum The cavity above a finished ceiling, where *luminaires* are *recessed*.

Portable lamp Any *luminaire* that is not permanently fixed to its source of power.

Projector A lighting unit which, by means of lenses and mirrors, concentrates light in a limited angle and intensifies it.

Rated life *Lamp* life based on a large sample batch; 50 per cent to fail earlier and 50 per cent to fail later than mean.

Recessed luminaire A fixture mounted above a ceiling (or other surface), with its opening at that surface.

Reflectance Ratio of the incident (arriving) light to the reflected (leaving) light.

Reflector A device used to direct the light from a source.

Scotopic vision The eye's ability to adapt to darkness.

Self-ballasted lamp A mercury *lamp* with an integral tungsten filament, to limit the current so no separate *ballast* is needed, and to blend the colors of mercury and tungsten.

Shielding A general term used to describe devices that block, diffuse, or redirect light, such as a *louvre* or lampshade.

Silver bowl lamp An *incandescent filament lamp* with a mirror finish on half the *bulb*, to provide indirect distribution of light.

Spectral A term generally applied to color or wavelength.

Specular relector A highly reflective surface, such as a mirror; one where the angle of the incident light and that of the reflected light are equal.

Spill light A term applied to any stray light outside the main concentration of the beam; usually controlled by louvres, baffles, and barn door accessories.

Starter gear see *Ballast*.

Step-down transformer A *transformer* that delivers a lower voltage to the output, as in low-voltage lighting.

Surface-mounted luminaire A fixture mounted directly on the ceiling or other surface.

Suspended (pendant) luminaire One that is hung from the ceiling using cable or rods.

Task lighting Purposeful lighting of a *work plane*.

Task plane see *Work plane*.

Torchere An indirect floor *lamp*, emitting most of its light upwards.

Transformer A device that changes the incoming (primary) voltage and delivers a different (secondary) voltage to the output.

Transmission The process by which incident (arriving) light passes through and leaves a medium, modified according to the surface: for instance, diffuse transmission from a translucent glass globe, regular transmission from a transparent glass globe, or selective spectral transmission as from a colored traffic light.

Tungsten halogen lamp A compact *incandescent filament lamp*, filled in part with halogen vapor.

Veiling reflection *Glare*, where *reflection* reduces *contrast* and so prevents detail being discerned.

Visual field That which can be perceived with the head and eyes in a fixed position.

Watts The unit of electrical energy.

Wavelength The distance between one peak or crest of a wave and the next corresponding peak or crest; can be applied to heat, light, sound, or other electro-magnetic waves.

Work plane Usually the horizontal surface at which a task is performed, and at which lght levels are specified and measured.

I·N·D·E·X

A·D·D·R·E·S·S·E·S

There are hundreds of companies manufacturing equipment for the lighting industry. They all have catalogues, some more available than others. A good lighting showroom should have a number of different catalogues for you to look at, not necessarily have. Below are a representative sample of manufacturers, who can direct you to your local representative.

LAMP MANUFACTURERS

General Electric Company
Nela Park
Cleveland, Ohio 44112
(216) 266–2121

GTE/Sylvania Lighting
Sylvania Lighting Center
Danvers, MA 01923
(617) 777–1900

Philips Lighting Corporation
Bank Street
Hightstown, NJ 08520
(609) 448–4000

Osram
PO Box 7062
Jeanne Drive
Newburgh, NY 12550
(914) 564–6300

Duro Test
2321 Kennedy Boulevard
North Bergen, NJ 07047
(201) 867–7000

ARCHITECTURAL FIXTURES

Lightolier
346 Claremont Avenue
Jersey City, NJ 07305
(212) 349–3100

Capri Lighting
6430 E. Slauson Avenue
Los Angeles, CA 90040
(213) 726–1800

Halo Lighting Division
400 Busse Road
Elk Grove Village, IL 60007
(312) 956–8400

Staff
PO Box 1020
Route 9w North
Highland, NY 12528
(914) 691–6262

FLUORESCENT FIXTURES

Legion Lighting Company, Inc.
221 Glenmore Avenue
Brooklyn, NY 11207
(718) 498–1770

Alkco
11500 W. Melrose Street
Franklin Park, IL 60131
(312) 451–0700

Columbia Lighting
PO Box 2787
Spokane, WA 99220
(509) 924–7000

OUTDOOR FIXTURES

Bega/FS
PO Box 50442
Santa Barbara, CA 93150
(805) 969–7721

Nightscaping by Loran
1705 E. Colton Avenue
Redlands, CA 92373
(714) 794–2121

Kim Lighting
16555 E. Gale Avenue
City of Industry, CA 91749
(818) 968–5666

DISPLAY FIXTURES

Litelab Corp.
251 Elm Street
Buffalo, NY 14203
(716) 856–4300

Lighting Services, Inc.
150 E. 58th Street
New York, NY 10155
(212) 838–8633

DECORATIVE FIXTURES

Atelier International, Ltd.
International Design Center
30–20 Thomson Avenue
Long Island City, NY 11101
(718) 392–0300

Artemide
150 E. 58th Street
New York, NY 10155
(212) 980–0710

Lazin Lighting, Inc.
53 Greene Street
New York, NY 10013
(212) 219–3888

CONTROLS

Lutron Electronics Company, Inc.
Suter Road, Box 205
Coopersburg, PA 18036
(215) 282–3800

Leviton Manufacturing Company, Inc.
59–25 Little Neck Parkway
Little Neck, NY 11362
(718) 229–4040

Prescolite
Lite Controls
1206 Tappan Circle
Carrollton, TX 75006
(214) 242–6581

A·C·K·N·O·W·L·E·D·G·M·E·N·T·S

All the artwork in this book was done by Hayward and Martin.

The letters next to each entry mean the following: *P* Photographer; *D* Designer; *L* Lighting; *A* Architect; *M* Manufacturer; *F* Fitting name; *S* Supplier.

Front cover: *P* Geoff Dann. Our thanks to Concord, Christopher Wray, Lutron, Argon, and John Cullen for the loan of equipment.

2 *P* Michael Dunne.
7 *P* ESTO/Peter Aaron.
10 *P* Norman McGrath.
13 *1–5 P* Geoff Dann.
16 *P* Michael Dunne; *A* Alan Buchsbaum.
19 *1–7 P* Geoff Dann; *D* Lindsay B; *S* The Cocktail Shop, London WC2.
21 *P* Michael Dunne.
22 *P* Michael Dunne; *L* Edward Effron.
23 *P* Michael Dunne; *L* Edward Effron
24 *1–3 P* Michael Dunne; *L* Edward Effron
27 *P* Michael Dunne
28 *P* Michael Dunne
29 *P* Daniel Eifert; *D* Rubén de Saavedra Ltd.
30 *P* Elizabeth Whiting Associates/ A. von Einsiedel.
31 top *P* Norman McGrath; bottom left *S* Kingston Industries; bottom right *P/L* Edward Effron.
32 *D* Mary Fox Linton; *L* Mole Richardson.
33 *P* Michael Dunne.
34 top *S* Colortran; bottom *P* Elizabeth Whiting Associates/T. Street-Porter, *A* Moore, Ruble & Yudell.
35 top *D* Gary Knibbs for XL Design Ltd.; bottom *P/L* Edward Effron.
37 *P* Arcaid/Richard Bryant; *A* Charles Jencks.

38–9 *P* Carla de Benedetti.
40 *P* Arcaid/Richard Bryant; *A* Gwathmey Siegel & Assocs.
41 top *P* Elizabeth Whiting Associates/Michael Dunne, *D* Borus & Borus; bottom *P* Daniel Eifert, *D* Rubén de Saavedra Ltd.
42 *P/L* Edward Effron.
43 *P* Michael Dunne.
44 *P* Robert Perron; *A* Louis Mackel.
45 *P* Ken Kirkwood for *English Style* by Suzanne Slesin and Stafford Cliff; *D* Johnny Grey.
46 *D* Gary Knibbs for XL Design Ltd.
47 *P* Arcaid/Richard Bryant; *A* Charles Jencks.
49 *P* Michael Dunne.
50 *P* Ken Kirkwood; *D* John Wright.
51 *P* Norman McGrath.
53 *P* Michael Dunne.
54 top and bottom *P* Norman McGrath.
55 top left *M* Brilliantleuchten, *F* 99078, 99097, 99050; top center *M* Habitat, *F* Box of toys; top right *S* Loucraine Broxton & Partners, *F* Gladys Goose; bottom *P* Michael Dunne, *L* Edward Effron.
56 *P/L* Edward Effron.
57 *P* Arcaid/Lucinda Lambton.
58 *P* James Mortimer © Frances Lincoln Ltd.
59 *P* Elliot Fine.
60 *P* Arcaid/Lucinda Lambton.
61 *P* Camera Press.
62 *S* Spectrum.
63 *P* Michael Dunne.
64 top *P* Concord Lighting Ltd.; bottom *D* Gary Knibbs for XL Design Ltd.
65 *P/L* Edward Effron; *D* Martin Lipsitt.
66–7 *P* Arcaid/Richard Bryant; *A* Eva Jiricna.
68 *P* ZEFA.
69 left *M* Lightolier, *F* 6496, 6499; right *P/L* Edward Effron, *D* Martin Lipsitt.
70 *P* Raak Lighting Architecture.

71 *P* Ron Sutherland © Frances Lincoln Ltd.; *D* Anthony Paul.
72 *P* Gary Rogers.
73 *P* Michael Dunne.
74 *P* Geoff Dann.
76 *M* Sylvania/GTE Lighting Products.
88 *M* Sylvania/GTE Lighting Products.
89 *P* Geoff Dann.
92 Chart based on information supplied by General Electric.
94 *1 P* Geoff Dann; *2 M* Spectrum, *F* Low energy metal halide spotlight; *3 M* ERCO, *F* 77601; *4 M* Concord, *F* MBF.
95 *P* Camera Press.
99 *1–4 P* Geoff Dann.
105 *P* Robert Perron.
107 *4 M* Mole Richardson, *F* MR 16 LO; *5 M* Concord, *F* 0862; *6 M* Edison Halo, *F* 591; *7 M* Concord, *F* 08760.
109 *3 M* ERCO; *4 M* Kotzolt; *5 M* C&R Lighting Systems, *F* 516 Pulsar; *6 M* ERCO, *F* 77770.
110–11 *M* Artemide.
112 *1 M* Raak, *F* Homeflood; *2 M* Raak, *F* Magnet Spot; *3 M* Raak, *F* Topical; *4 M* Raak, *F* Tube-lite; *5 M* Light, *F* Per Quatro.
113 *6 M* Raak, *F* F-3045, 4800; *7 M* Light, *F* PM 30; *8 M* Stilnovo, *F* Bulbo casa.
114 *2 M* Stilnovo, *F* Minibox; *3 M* Wotan, *F* Maxispot, Minispot, Agilok; *4 M* Maclamp, *F* BL Spot 4/1, BL Super 4/2.
115 *5 M* Stilnovo, *F* Tokio; *6 M* Lightolier, *F* 8535; *7 M* Lightolier, *F* 8536; *8 M* Marcatré, *F* 600; *9 M* Capri Lighting, *F* Odyssey.
116 *1 M* Brilliantleuchten, *F* Swanline Pendant; *2 M* Light, *F* Kings Profile; *3 M* Artemide, *F* Cyclos Sospensione.
117 *4 M* Artemide, *F* Area 50 a soliscundi; *5 M* Raak, *F* B1017.0000; *6 M* iGuzzini, *F* F3200, *S* Forma.

118 *1 M* Artemide, *F* Icaro;
2 M Brilliantleuchten, *F* Nite Lite;
3D Ferguson & Wheeler, *S* British
Home Stores; *4 M* Raak, *F* W1876.5000.
119 *5 M* Artemide, *F* Damocle;
6 M Christopher Wray, *F* Regal;
7 M Luci, *F* Danielle, *S* Candell Ltd.
120 *1 M* Brilliantleuchten, *F* Movie;
2 M Koch & Lowy Inc, *F* T423 clear
glass light; *3 M* Christopher Wray,
F Hefner lamp.
121 *4 M* Nobilis-Fontan, *F* 23;
5 M Flos, *F* Biagio; *6 M* Griffin,
F Windsor; *7 M* Leucos, *F* Tiki,
S Forma.
122 *1 M* Artemide, *F* Tizio;
2 M Stilnovo, *F* Nastro; *3 M* Ledu,
F C10D; *4 M* Light, *F* PM 50P.
123 *5 M* Brilliantleuchten, *F* Smal
125 46/05; *6 M* Artemide, *F* Sintesi
professionale; *7 M* Wotan.
124 *1 M* Flos, *F* Papillona,
S Marcatré; *2 M* Flos, *F* Parentesi,
S Marcatré; *3 M* Artemide, *F* Tizio;
4 M Cil, *F* Quattro, *S* Forma.
125 *5 M* Arteluce, *F* Jill, *S* Marcatré;
6 M Brilliantleuchten, *F* Smal 12555;
7 M Flos, *F* Arco, *S* Marcatré.
126 *1 M* Flos, *F* Tamburo, *F* Copilot.

S Marcatré; *2M* Concord/Bega,
F 9872; *3 M* Hoffmeister,
F 0.77037.41-695; *4 M* Stilnovo
F Bulbo; *5 M* Brilliantleuchten,
F Starlight.
127 *6 M* Raak, *F* S 2239.0000;
7 M Tivoli, *F* Tivoli Tubing;
8 M Concord/Bega, *F* 2572;
9 M Concord/Bega, *F* 2874.
129 *4 M* Concord, *F* Targa.
130 *1 M* Lutron, *F* Nova
incandescent dimmer; *2 M* Litestat,
F Touchlite Imperial range T1;
3 M Litestat, *F* English range EPI;
4 M Lutron, *F* Ampion fluorescent
240-volt dimmer; *5 M* Relco,
F RT80, RT32, RT88, RT1.
131 *6 M* Litestat, *F* Touchlite
Imperial range T1; *7 M* Home
Automation, *F* Time lag control;
8 M Home Automation,
F SC400 WILS; *9 M* Home
Automation, *F* RB 100 W Black box
security switch; *10 M* Diablo,
F Security switch; *11 M* Home
Automation; *F* Ripul remote
controller; *12 M* Leviton, *F* Central
control system.

Frances Lincoln Limited would like to thank the following people and organizations for their special help in the preparation of this book.

For allowing their houses to be photographed: Mrs T. Bardega, Janey and Caradoc King, Martin Summers, Tony Tooth. For location research: Linda Martin, Sue Gladstone. For supplying advice and equipment: Philips Electronics (Lighting Division), Thorn EMI, Concord Lighting Limited, Wotan Lamps Limited. Thanks also to Peter Burian for checking the text, to Hayward and Martin for the artwork, to Richard and Hilary Bird for the index, to Eva Jiricna for valuable information, to Barry Randell of Vantage Photosetting, to Dawn Stevenson and Steve Talbot of DSCI, to Louise Tucker for help with the design, to Amanda Malpass for typing, and to Pippa Rubinstein for initial work on the project.

Editor Sybil del Strother
Art editor Judith Robertson

Picture research Anne Fraser

Art direction Steven Wooster

Typesetting
Best-set Typesetter Ltd.
Hong Kong

Reproduction
D.S. Colour International Ltd.